HOW TO PLAY WINNING POKER

"In compelling and easy-to-understand language, Avery Cardoza maps out a powerful path to poker profit. This book is packed with practical tips and penetrating insight."
— Mike Caro, the legendary Mad Genius of Poker

"Avery Cardoza is the expert at leading new and slightly experienced poker players to the winner's circle. His advice on playing hold'em in both cash games and tournaments is priceless."
— Tom McEvoy, 1983 World Champion of Poker, "Champion of the Champions"

Cardoza's 'Twenty-One Essential Winning Concepts' is one of the most important chapters in poker literature for the average player. The rest of the book is solid gold, however this advice alone is well worth the cost by itself."
— Shane Smith, author *Tournament Tips from the Poker Pros*

HOW TO PLAY
WINNING
POKER

AVERY CARDOZA

CARDOZA PUBLISHING

Cardoza Publishing is the foremost gaming and gambling publisher in the world with a library of more than 200 up-to-date and easy-to-read books and strategies. These authoritative works are written by the top experts in their fields and with more than 10,000,000 books in print, represent the best-selling and most popular gaming books anywhere.

SIXTH EDITION

New Edition Copyright© 2009 by Avery Cardoza
-All Rights Reserved-

Library of Congress Catalog Card No: 2009933891
ISBN 13: 978-1-5804-2236-9
ISBN 10: 1-58042-236-5

About the Author

Avery Cardoza is the world's foremost authority on gambling and a multimillion-selling author of twenty-one books. Millions of players have learned how to play and win money gambling following his no-nonsense practical advice. His poker books include *The Basics of Winning Poker, The Basics of Winning Hold'em Poker, Poker Talk: How to Talk Poker Like a Pro, How to Play Winning Poker,* and *Crash Course in Beating Texas Hold'em Poker.*

He is a frequent money-winner and regular player in the World Series of Poker and the high stakes poker tournaments seen on television. Cardoza has crippled the stacks of, or eliminated, more than a dozen world champions from major tournament competitions.

Visit www.cardozabooks.com for a full list of Cardoza Publishing books.

TABLE OF CONTENTS

1. INTRODUCTION

Poker is the greatest and most exciting gambling game. It's an American tradition enjoyed by rich and poor, men and women of all classes who gather around a table and vie for stakes ranging from mere pennies to millions of dollars. No other game combines skill, luck, and psychology with the drama of the bluff in such a fascinating weave.

This completely revised new edition contains coverage of today's hot new game, Texas hold'em poker, including advice and winning strategies for no-limit hold'em—both cash games and tournaments—as well as limit hold'em cash games waiting like ripe fruit for you to enjoy.

New chapters also include information on how to get started in the profitable poker games played online and how to join the exciting new world of poker tournaments—both local events where you can pocket thousands or tens of thousands of dollars and the big televised events where a good run can win you more than a million dollars and everlasting fame. We'll cover strategies for every stage of a tournament and insider advice that will give you a legitimate chance of becoming a champion.

This book will show you how be a winner at all the major poker games: hold'em (no-limit, pot-limit, and limit), seven-card stud (high, high-low, and razz), draw poker (jacks or better, anything opens, lowball, and triple draw) and Omaha (high and high-low eight-or-better). You'll learn the rules and basics of each game, how to play high, low, and high-low poker, the differences between cardroom and private games, betting options, and everything else you need to be an informed player. Hard-hitting strategies and key concepts are included for every game so you can go out there right away and mix it up.

You'll also benefit from expanded general strategy chapters—powerful poker concepts and advice that will take your game up many notches—as well as twenty-one essential winning concepts, fifteen fundamental concepts for bluffing, and a brutally honest chapter on playing poker professionally.

You'll also learn the following:

• How to recognize monster, leading, trailing, and weak hands, and how to play these hand-types for maximum profits and minimal losses.

• How to take advantage of good position at the table to leverage opponents out of pots.

• How to use pot odds and implied odds to determine the soundness of a bet.

INTRODUCTION

• How to read your opponents' playing styles and cash in on the information they give you.

• Other key concepts essential for correct decision making at poker.

There is a lot to learn and lots of money to be made playing good poker. Read on, my friend, so you can get your share of the pie!

2. HISTORY

ORIGINS

Poker is a truly great gambling game whose popularity seems to grow with time. It flourishes in private homes and cardrooms throughout the United States and Canada, and it has devotees around the world as well. For many players, the Friday night poker game has been an uninterrupted ritual for years.

The first seeds of modern poker drifted across the oceans from the European and Asian continents in the early 1800s. Card games from Persia (As Nas or As), France (Poque) and Germany (Pochen or Poch) are credited as being the forerunners of poker. This new gambling game was cultivated in and around the burgeoning Mississippi River port of New Orleans. The Louisiana Purchase of 1803 opened up a wild and new frontier, and soon thereafter, poker began to capture the gambling spirits and imagination of the new settlers.

The original American poker game used only a 20-card deck of four suits: spades, diamonds, clubs and hearts. The deck contained four each of aces, kings, queens, jacks, and tens, one ordinal per suit. This early form did not recognize straights and flushes.

By the 1840s, the full 52-card deck had been adopted, with the four suits now represented in card values of aces (high) through deuces (low). Straights and flushes made their way into the game by the late 1850s, establishing the basic modern-day form of poker.

THE MODERN AGE OF POKER

The modern age of poker dates back just a few years, when two major events catapulted poker to the forefront of the American consciousness.

The major catalyst to this boom took place in March of 2003, when the first televised showing of the World Poker Tour on the Travel Channel hit the airwaves. The featured game was no-limit Texas hold'em, the exciting but obscure version of poker in which players could bet all their chips on one hand. The program showed the players hole cards to the television audience—something that had never been done before—so viewers could follow the tension as the hand was being played.

This innovation captivated the audience so much, that five million viewers a week flocked to this new and exciting programming. In fact, the broadcasts were so successful that reruns attracted a larger audience than the original showings and became the Travel Channel's number one show.

HISTORY

The second watershed event occurred when an obscure accountant from Tennessee invested $40 in an online tournament, won a seat to the World Series of Poker, and parlayed that satellite win into first place in the hallowed grounds of poker's official championship. Not only would the improbably named Chris Moneymaker's life never be the same, but neither would the game of poker. Moneymaker outlasted a field of the world's greatest players to take the championship—and $2.5 million!

Suddenly, the game which had been dying in cardrooms across the country, got hot and enjoyed a popularity never before seen. And not just in the United States, but in countries around the world. The craze jumped over the ocean, and countries which never really had much of a poker culture embraced this American game with a passion. England, Sweden, France, Australia (home to the 2005 World Champion), and a host of other countries jumped into the game while fanatics flocked to online sites, live tournaments and cash games wherever they could find them.

"Hey," people thought, "if Moneymaker can win all that money, so can I." And it was true. While the skilled players were clearly the favorites in a contest, every player had a shot at winning the big one as witnessed by the world championships in 2004 and 2005, when two more unknown players captured the coveted World Championship titles, a trend that continues even today.

A new breed of celebrity came to the public's consciousness, the collection of sunglass-wearing oddballs who were capturing major titles and strutting their piles of chips and bluffs on national television. And poker stars who had been obscure just a few years earlier became household names.

The new age of poker was born.

3. TYPES OF POKER GAMES

Poker can be played in two basic forms—as cash games or in a tournament format.

CASH GAMES

In a **cash game**, the chips you play with represent real money. If you go broke, you can always dig in to your pocket for more money. If you give the poker room $200 in cash, you get $200 worth of chips in return. If you build it up to $375, you can quit and convert your chips to cash anytime you want.

A cash game with seven or more players is known as a **ring game**. Six players or fewer is considered **short-handed**. And when there are just two players going against one another, it is called a **head-to-head** or **heads-up** game.

Your goal in a cash game is to win as much money as you can, or if things are going poorly, to lose as little as possible.

TOURNAMENTS

In a **tournament**, every player starts with an equal number of chips and plays until one player holds them all. As players lose their chips, they are eliminated from the tournament. Your goal in a tournament is to survive as long as you can. At the very least, you want to survive long enough to earn prizes, usually money, and in the best case scenario, to become the champion, and capture the biggest prize.

LIMIT, NO-LIMIT, AND POT-LIMIT

Poker has three different types of betting structures: limit, pot-limit, and no-limit. These structures don't change the basic way the games are played, only the amount of money that can be bet. The big difference between the three structures is the strategy. The amount you can bet changes the hands that you should play, when you should play them, and how much you should risk in any given situation.

In cardrooms, you'll find the betting limits posted at the table, or you will be directed to the game of your choice by the casino personnel. In private games, the betting limits are prearranged and agreed upon by the players in advance or on the spot, but always before the cards are dealt.

Let's take a brief look at each betting structure.

TYPES OF POKER GAMES

LIMIT POKER

In **limit** poker, the most common game played in card-rooms and casinos for cash, all bets are divided into a two-tier structure, such as $1/$2, $3/$6, $5/$10, $10/$20, and $15/$30, with the larger limit bets being exactly double the lower limit. In the early betting round, all bets and raises must be at the lower limit, and in the later rounds, all bets double and are made at the higher limit. In a $5/$10 limit game, for example, when the lower limit of betting is in effect, all bets and raises must be in $5 increments. When the upper range is in effect, all bets and raises must be in $10 increments.

Unless a player is short-stacked and cannot meet the required amount, all bets must be at the preestablished limits of the game.

One form of limit poker, called **spread-limit**, allows you to bet any amount between the minimum and maximum amounts specified for the game. Spread limit is typically played in very low stakes games. For example, in a $1-$5 game, you may bet or raise $1, $2, $3, $4, or $5 on any betting round. There is also a $1-$4-$8 spread-limit format where all bets in the early betting rounds can be anywhere from $1 to $4, and in the later betting rounds, from $1 to $8.

In the sections on the individual games, we will go over exactly when the upper level of betting comes into effect and how that works.

NO-LIMIT POKER

No-limit hold'em is the exciting no-holds barred style of poker played in the World Series of Poker main event and seen on television by millions weekly on the World Poker Tour and stations such as the Travel Channel and ESPN. No-limit is usually associated with Texas hold'em, but this style of betting can be played in any variation.

The prevailing feature of no-limit poker is that you can bet any amount up to what you have in front of you on the table anytime it is your turn. That exciting all-in call signals a player's intention to put all his chips on the line.

POT-LIMIT POKER

Pot-limit is most often associated with hold'em and Omaha, though this betting structure, like no-limit, can be played with any poker variation. The minimum bet allowed in pot-limit is that of the big blind bet (which helps determine the size of the game), while the maximum bet allowed is defined by the size of the pot. For example, if $75 is currently in the pot, then $75 is the maximum bet allowed.

As you can see, the pot sizes in pot-limit quickly spiral to large amounts. Like no-limit, this betting structure is not for the timid.

4. THE BASICS OF POKER

OBJECT OF THE GAME

Your object in poker is to win the money in the **pot**, the accumulation of bets and antes in the center of the table. You can win in two ways. The first way is to have the highest ranking hand at the **showdown**—the final act in poker, where all active players' hands are revealed to see who has the best one. The second way is to be the last player remaining when all other players have dropped out of play. When this occurs, there is no showdown, and you automatically win the pot.

WINNING POTS

You can win only what your opponents risk, so pots will be of different sizes. They will vary from small ones, in which players have hands they are not willing to commit many chips to, to large ones where two or more players have strong hands they think will win and will push chips at each other to build the pot or induce opponents to fold and bow out of the hand.

Do not confuse the goal of winning chips with winning pots. It is not how many pots you win, but how much money. It is better to win one pot with $500 in chips than three pots with $100 each. In fact, the player who wins the most pots often ends up a loser! Why? He's playing too many hands, and while he's winning a lot of them, at the same time, he is losing a lot of other hands and for a lot of chips since he is paying to see these hands through to the end. When those hands don't win, small losses quickly add up to big ones.

PARTICIPANTS

Poker can be played with as few as two players to as many as the 52-card deck can support, usually anywhere from eight to ten players, depending on the variation played. For example, seven-card stud will usually be played eight-handed, and hold'em nine- or ten-handed. In fact, hold'em, can theoretically support as many as twenty-two players in a live game, though games with more than ten players are rarely seen in any poker variation.

In a private game, one of the players is designated as the **dealer**, the person who shuffles and deals the cards to the players. The dealer position changes with each hand, rotating around the table in a clockwise direction, with each player having a chance to deal. The dealer is still an active player in a private game and enjoys no advantage other than any positional edge he may have for the particular game played.

In a casino or cardroom, the house will supply a dealer. He is not a participant in the betting or play of the game. His role is simply to shuffle the deck, deal the cards, and direct the action so that the game runs smoothly. He will point out whose turn it is to play and pull bets into the pot after each round of cards. And at the showdown, he will announce the best hand, push the pot over to the winning player, then reshuffle the cards, and get ready for the next deal.

In casino variations in which the dealer enjoys a positional advantage, such as hold'em, lowball, Omaha, and draw poker, a **button** is utilized to designate the dealer's imaginary position. The button rotates around the table, one spot at a time, in clockwise fashion, so that, as in the private game, each player has a chance to enjoy the advantages of acting last.

Poker is a game where every participant plays by himself and for himself alone against all other players. Collusion and partnership play are both illegal and considered cheating.

THE CARDROOM MANAGER OR TOURNAMENT DIRECTOR

In a cardroom, the employee responsible for the supervision of poker games is the **cardroom manager**, or if there is a tournament in progress, the **tournament director**. When a dispute arises, the dealer or one of the players may call over the supervisor for a ruling. If a player gets out of hand and abusive, the supervisors may ask the player to act more appropriately and let that serve as a warning. If the situation warrants or the abuse or infractions of the rules or decorum of the game continues, the player may be given a "time out," and will be disallowed from play for say, ten or twenty minutes, twenty-four hours, or in extreme cases, permanently.

THE POKER TABLE

In a cardroom, the players and dealer sit around a table built to accommodate the game of poker. The dealer sits in the middle of the long side where there is an indentation cut into the table to facilitate access to the players. He will usually have a small rack in front of him where he can keep an extra deck of cards, chips, cash, and a few other items. In a cash game, he may also have a drop box where he will deposit money taken out of the pot as the house commission (see "Rake," later).

THE DECK OF CARDS

Poker is played with a standard pack of fifty-two cards consisting of thirteen ranks, ace through king in each of four suits (hearts, clubs, diamonds, spades). The ace is the best and highest card, followed in descending order by the king, queen, jack, 10, 9, 8, 7, 6, 5, 4, 3, and then the **deuce** or 2, which is the lowest ranked card. The king, queen, and jack are known as **picture cards** or **face cards**.

When the cards are held together in various combinations, they form hands of different strengths. These are called **hand rankings** or **poker rankings**.

THE BASICS OF POKER

The Four Suits

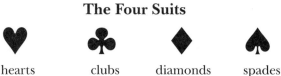

hearts clubs diamonds spades

The four suits in poker have no basic value in the determination of winning hands. As you shall see, it is not the value of the individual cards that reigns supreme in poker, but the combination of cards which determine the value of a player's hand.

CARD ABBREVIATIONS

Cards are referred to in writing by the following commonly used symbols: ace (A), king (K), queen (Q), jack (J), and all others directly by their numerical value, 10, 9, 8, 7, 6, 5, 4, 3, and 2.

RANK OF HANDS: HIGH POKER

Poker is generally played as high poker. The best hand you can hold is the royal flush, followed by a straight flush, four of a kind, full house, flush, straight, three of a kind, two pair, one pair, and high card hand. The order in which cards are dealt or how they are displayed is irrelevant to the final value of the hand. For example, 7-7-K-A-5 is equivalent to A-K-7-7-5.

Listed here are the rankings of hands in ascending order, from worst to best. Each hand beats all those previously listed. Also note that all poker hands consist of five cards, regardless of the variation played.

HIGH CARD

A hand containing five unmatched cards, that is, lacking any of the combinations shown below, is valued by its highest ranking card. For example, A-10-9-8-7 is considered an "ace-high" hand. It beats the lesser "king-high" hand of K-Q-J-4-3.

King-High Hand

When the highest ranking cards are identical, the next highest card wins. If this too is equivalent, then the next highest is compared and so on through the fifth card. The hand K-Q-7-5-2 beats K-Q-7-4-3. If all cards are identical, the hand is a draw, and the pot is split.

ONE PAIR

A hand with one set of identically valued cards, along with three unmatched cards is called a **pair**. The hand 2-2-8-4-A is called "a pair of twos." Pairs are ranked in order of value from aces (the highest) down to deuces (the lowest). Thus, a pair of aces beats a pair of kings, and a pair of nines is better than a pair of sixes.

One Pair

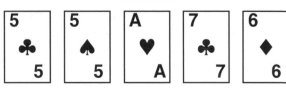

When two players hold equally paired hands, the highest odd card or **kicker** decides the winner. For example, 8-8-Q-7-3 beats 8-8-J-9-7. If the highest unmatched cards are also equivalently valued, then the next highest cards are compared, and then the last cards if necessary. J-J-10-9-8 beats J-J-10-9-7. If all cards are identical, the hand is a tie and the pot is split.

TWO PAIR

A hand with two sets of equivalently valued or "paired" cards, along with an unmatched card, is called **two pair**. 10-10-8-8-5 is a two-pair hand called "tens up" or "tens over eights," since the tens are the higher ranking pair. Similarly, A-A-3-3-J is called "aces up" or "aces over threes."

Two Pair

If more than one player holds a two-pair hand, the winner would be the player holding the higher ranked of the top pair. For example, J-J-7-7-K beats 10-10-9-9-A. When the higher ranking pairs are identical, the next pair is compared to determine the winner. 8-8-5-5-9 beats 8-8-4-4-10. When both pairs are evenly matched, the higher ranking fifth card—the kicker—determines the victor. K-K-J-J-A beats K-K-J-J-4. If all cards are equally ranked, such as 5-5-3-3-2 and 5-5-3-3-2, then the hand is a tie and the pot is split.

THREE OF A KIND

A hand of three matched cards of identical rank along with two unmatched cards is called a **three of a kind**, **triplets**, **trips,** or a **set**. 7-7-7-Q-2 is called "three sevens" or "a set of sevens."

Three of a Kind

When two players hold a set, the player with the higher ranking three-of-a-kind takes the pot. J-J-J-3-4 is higher ranked than 8-8-8-Q-5. If two identically ranked three of a kind hands are competing, then the highest odd card determines the winner. 9-9-9-J-4 beats 9-9-9-8-5 and 9-9-9-J-3.

STRAIGHT

A hand of five non-suited cards in sequential order, such as 10-9-8-7-6, is called a **straight**. When straights contain an ace, the ace must serve as either the highest card in the run—such as the ace-high straight A-K-Q-J-10—or the lowest card—as in the 5-high straight 5-4-3-2-A. The ace in the latter hand is a low card since it is at the bottom of the sequence. The hand Q-K-A-2-3 is not a straight. It's merely an ace-high hand. Even a lowly pair beats it.

Straight

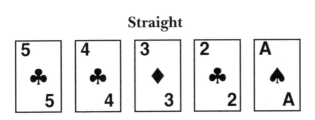

When two or more straights are in competition, the straight with the highest ranking card takes the pot. A 9-high straight beats out a 7-high straight. When two straights share the highest ranking card, the hand is a tie and the pot is split.

FLUSH

Any five cards of the same suit constitutes a **flush**. A hand of A♠ K♠ 7♠ 3♠ 2♠ is called an ace-high flush in spades, and Q♥ 10♥ 7♥ 5♥ 3♥ is a queen-high flush in hearts. When two or more players hold flushes, the flush with the highest ranking card wins the pot. In the above example, the ace-high flush holds the higher ranking card (the ace) and is therefore the stronger hand.

Flush

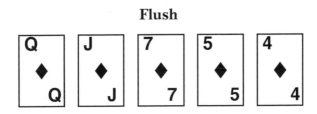

If the highest ranking cards in competing flushes are of equivalent rank, the next highest card decides the winner. If they too are tied, then the next cards, and so on, down to the fifth card if need be.

For example, in the two flushes K♦ Q♦ 9♦ 7♦ 6♦ and K♥ Q♥ J♥ 5♥ 2♥, the heart flush is the stronger flush, since its third highest ranking card, the jack, is higher ranking than the 9 of the diamond flush.

When all five cards of competing flushes are identical, the hand is a tie, and the winners split the pot. Suits are irrelevant in determining the ranking of a flush.

FULL HOUSE

A **full house** consists of three cards of identical rank along with two cards of an identical but different rank—that is, a three of a kind and a pair together. 3-3-3-A-A and 5-5-5-7-7 are two examples of full houses.

Full House

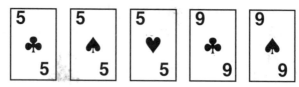

When two players hold full houses, the hand holding the higher ranking three of a kind will win the pot. In the above example, the 5-5-5-7-7 full house is higher ranking than the 3-3-3-A-A. If both players hold the same five cards, it is a tie.

FOUR OF A KIND

Four cards of identical rank, such as the hand J-J-J-J-3, is called a **four of a kind** or **quads**, and is almost a sure win in straight poker (poker without a wild card). The odd card in the above example, the 3, is irrelevant unless another player holds the same quads, in which case the highest odd card will determine the winner. If two players hold quads, the higher ranking four of a kind will win the hand. For example, J-J-J-J-3 beats out both 7-7-7-7-A and J-J-J-J-2.

Four of a Kind

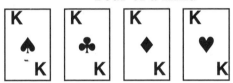

STRAIGHT FLUSH

Five cards of the same suit in numerical sequence, such as Q♦ J♦ 10♦ 9♦ 8♦, is called a **straight flush**. This particular example is called a queen-high straight flush, since the queen is the highest ranking card. The straight flush is the second most powerful hand in poker played without wild cards.

Straight Flush

When two straight flushes are in competition for the pot, the straight flush with the highest ranking card wins. For example, a queen-high straight flush beats a 10-high straight flush. If two players hold equivalently ranked straight flushes, such as 9♣ 8♣ 7♣ 6♣ 5♣ and 9♥ 8♥ 7♥ 6♥ 5♥, then the hand is a tie and the pot is split. Suits have no dominance over one another in poker.

The ace can be used as either the highest card in the straight flush (an ace-high hand being a royal flush) or the lowest card, as in A♦ 2♦ 3♦ 4♦ 5♦. Straight flushes may not wrap around the ace. For example, the hand of Q♣ K♣ A♣ 2♣ 3♣ is not a straight flush. It's simply a flush.

ROYAL FLUSH

A hand of A-K-Q-J-10, all in the same suit, is called a **royal flush**. For example, A♠ K♠ Q♠ J♠ 10♠ is a royal flush. The royal flush is the most powerful and rarest hand in poker, a thing of beauty that a player will rarely, if ever, see in a lifetime of play. In the extremely unlikely event that two players hold royal flushes, the hand is a tie and the pot is split.

Royal Flush

A ♦ A	K ♦ K	Q ♦ Q	J ♦ J	10 ♦ 10

POKER PROBABILITIES

There are a total of 2,598,960 five-card combinations possible with a 52-card deck. The following chart illustrates the chances of receiving each type of hand in the first five cards dealt.

Probabilities of Five-Card Poker Hands		
Hand	**Number**	**Approximate Odds**
Royal Flush	4	649,740 to 1
Straight Flush	36	72,192 to 1
Four of a Kind*	624	4,164 to 1
Full House	3,744	693 to 1
Flush	5,108	508 to 1
Straight	10,200	254 to 1
Three of a Kind	54,912	46 to 1
Two Pair	123,552	20 to 1
One Pair	1,098,240	1.37 to 1
No Hand	1,302,540	1 to 1

*Though there are only 13 four-of-a-kind combinations, to be accurate, this calculation must include the total number of possibilities when the fifth card is figured in to make a five-card hand.

WILD CARDS

In some home poker games, players designate certain cards as **wild cards**. These are cards which can take on any value and suit at the holder's discretion, even as a duplicate of a card already held. Sometimes the "53rd" and "54th" cards of the deck, the jokers, are used as wild cards. Players might also designate the deuces or the one-eyed jacks as wild cards. Any card can be considered wild with the consent of all players.

If the deuces were used as wild cards, for example, the hand 6-5-3-2-2 would be a straight by designating one deuce as a 7 and the other as a 4. At the showdown, the holder of this hand would represent a 7-high straight as his best combination.

RANK OF HANDS: WILD CARD POKER

The only difference in the ranking of hands in wild card poker from that of straight high poker is that a five of a kind hand—which is possible only in wild card

Ranks of Hands · Wild Card Poker

Five of a Kind
Royal Flush
Straight Flush
Four of a Kind
Full House
Flush
Straight
Three of a Kind
Two Pairs
One Pair
High Card

poker—is the highest ranking combination, above that of a royal flush. Otherwise, all other poker rankings, from the royal flush down to the high card, are equivalent.

On the previous page are the relative rankings of hands, from highest to lowest, in wild card poker.

RANK OF HANDS: LOW POKER

In **low poker**, the ranking of hands is the opposite to that of high poker, with the lowest hand being the most powerful and the highest hand being the least powerful. There are two varieties of low poker games: ace-to-five and deuce-to-seven.

In **ace-to-five**, the ace is considered the lowest and therefore most powerful card. The hand 5-4-3-2-A is the best low total possible with 6-4-3-2-A and 6-5-3-2-A being the next two best hands. Straights and flushes don't count against low hands.

In **deuce-to-seven** low poker, also known as **Kansas City lowball**, the 2 is the lowest and best card and the ace is the highest and worst. The hand 7-5-4-3-2 is the best possible hand, followed by 7-6-4-3-2 and 7-6-5-3-2. In this variation, unlike ace-to-five, straights and flushes count as high so you don't want to end up with hands such as 8-7-6-5-4 or 7-6-5-4-2 all in hearts.

See the sections on low poker for a further discussion of low poker rankings.

MONEY AND CHIPS

Poker is almost always played with **chips**, thin, circular clay or plastic units that are assigned specific values, such as $1, $5, $25, and $100. Poker can also be played for cash, but this is discouraged in cardrooms as it slows down the game. Chips are much more practical to use.

In casino poker, the standard denominations of chips are $1, $5, $25, $100, and sometimes $10 units as well. In big money games, you can find $1,000, $5,000, and if the game is big enough, $25,000 and $100,000 chips! While some casinos use their own color code, the standard color scheme of poker chips is: $1-blue or white, $5-red, $25-green, and $100-black.

To receive chips in a cardroom, give the dealer cash, and he'll give you back the equivalent value in chips. This exchange of cash for chips is called a **buy-in** and is usually done right at the table. Dealers will accept only cash for chips, so if you have traveler's checks, credit cards, or other forms of money, you need to exchange these for cash at the area marked **Casino Cashier**. Then, with cash in hand, you can return to the poker table and buy chips.

In private games, players generally use chips, though sometimes the game will be cash only. When chips are used, one player acts as the **bank** or **banker**. He converts players' cash buy-ins to equivalent values in chips. The most common denominations of chips used in private games are one unit, five units, ten units, twenty-five units, and one-hundred units. A unit can equal 1¢, $1, or whatever value is agreed upon by the players. Now, with the recent interest in poker, many home games are using casino style chips for their games.

PRELIMINARIES OF PLAY

The dealer is responsible for shuffling the cards after each round of play so that they are mixed well and in random order. In a private game, the players take turns dealing, and the deck will be offered to a player, usually on the dealer's right, for the **cut**. This player initiates the cut by removing the top part of the deck and placing it to one side, face down. The dealer completes the cut by placing the former lower portion of the deck on top of the former upper section, thereby making the deck of cards whole again.

To be valid, a cut must go deeper than the top five cards of the deck and may not go further in than the last five. This rule helps prevent players, who have inadvertently (or otherwise) seen the top or bottom cards, from using the cut to their advantage. A cut of any number of cards between these two extremes is valid.

In a cardroom, the dealer cuts the cards himself, using a **cut card**, a plastic card that is not part of the deck (and typically of a different and distinct color), to separate the deck into two stacks so that the top and bottom order of the packs can be reversed. This helps protect against cheating and covers the bottom card of the deck so that it is not accidentally exposed.

MANDATORY STARTING BETS

In poker, one or more players are typically required to put a bet into the pot before the cards are dealt. There are two types of mandatory bets: blinds and antes. **Blinds** are used in hold'em, Omaha, and some draw variations. They are generally required of the first two players to the left of the dealer position. An **ante**, also known as a **sweetener**, is a uniform and forced bet placed into the pot by all players before the cards are dealt. The sizes of the blinds and antes in home games are prearranged by the players. In a casino, they are set by the house. Antes are used in a majority of private poker games and some casino games.

Antes and blinds create an immediate pot in poker, giving players money to go after before the cards are even dealt. Players will frequently play forcefully in the early going, hoping to force opposing players out of the pot so they can pick up the antes and blinds without going further into a hand. Where there are blinds, as in hold'em and Omaha, this is called **stealing the blinds**. In ante games, it is called **stealing the ante**.

We'll cover the mechanics of the blind bets in greater detail in the appropriate game sections.

THE PLAY OF THE GAME

After the dealer shuffles the cards and offers the cut, the deal is ready to begin. If the game requires an ante, the dealer may announce "**ante-up**," a call for all players to place their antes into the pot. If you're playing hold'em or Omaha, the dealer will make sure that the blinds are posted before the cards are dealt.

The dealer begins by distributing cards to the player on his immediate left. He deals cards one at a time in a clockwise rotation, until each player has received the requisite number of cards for the poker variation being played. In casino games, where a rotating button is used to mark the dealer's position, the deal begins with the player to the left of the button and continues around the table in the same fashion as in private games.

Like the dealing of the cards, play always proceeds in a clockwise direction. The first round begins with the player sitting to the immediate left of the blinds, the dealer, or, in some stud games, with either the high or low card opening play. Play will continue around the table, until each player in turn has acted.

In later rounds, the first player to act depends on the variation being played. We'll cover the particulars of play under the sections on the games themselves.

THE PLAYER'S OPTIONS

When it is your turn to act, the following options, which apply to all forms of poker, are available to you:

    1. Bet: Put chips at risk, that is, wager money, if no player has done so before you.

    2. Call: Match a bet if one has already been placed before your turn.

3. Raise: Increase the size of a current bet such that opponents, including the original bettor, must put additional money into the pot to stay active in a hand.

4. Fold: Give up your cards and opt out of play if a bet is due and you do not wish to match it. This forfeits your chance of competing for the pot.

5. Check: Stay active in a hand without making a bet and risking chips. This is only possible if no bets have been made.

The first three options—bet, call, and raise—are all a form of putting chips at risk in hopes of winning the pot. Once chips are bet and due, you must match that bet to continue playing for the pot or you must fold. Checking is not an option. If no chips are due, you can stay active in the hand without cost by checking.

Once a bet has been made, each **active player**—one who has not folded—is faced with the same options: call, fold, or raise. Additionally, once placed, a bet no longer belongs to the bettor; it becomes the property of the pot, the communal collection of money that is up for grabs by all active players.

Betting continues in a round until the last bet or raise is called by all active players, at which point the betting round is over. A player may not raise his own bet when his betting turn comes around. He may raise only another player's bet or raise.

THE SHOWDOWN

If two or more players remain at the conclusion of all betting in the final betting round of a poker game, the showdown occurs. The **showdown** is the final act in a poker game where remaining players reveal their hands to determine the winner of the pot.

The player whose last bet or raise was called—if all players checked, the first to the left of the dealer position—turns over his cards first and reveals his hand. The player with the best hand at the showdown wins all the money in the pot. Players holding losing hands at the showdown may concede the pot without showing their cards.

In the event of a tie, or if there are two winners—as may be the case in high-low games—the pot is split evenly among those players.

If only one player remains after the final betting round, or at any point during the game, there is no showdown. The lone remaining player automatically wins the pot.

WHAT BETTING IS ALL ABOUT

In poker, you compete for the pot, which is kept in the middle of the table. You'll make bets for one of three reasons:

1. You feel your hand has enough strength to win and you want to induce opponents to put more money into the pot.

2. You want to force opponents out of the pot so that the field is narrowed, since fewer players increases your chances of winning.

3. You want to induce all your opponents to fold so that you can win the pot uncontested.

Playing Tip
Never fold a hand, no matter how bad, when you can check and remain active for free.

MINIMUM AND MAXIMUM BETS
LIMIT POKER

The minimum and maximum bets in limit games are strictly regulated according to the preset limits of the game. For example, $3/$6 and $5/$10 are two common limits. The number of raises allowed in a round are also restricted, usually limited to three or four total according to the house rules for the cardroom. In other words, if there is a three-raise limit and the action goes bet, raise, reraise, and reraise, the raising would be **capped**. No more raises would be allowed for that round.

The exception to this rule comes into play when players are heads-up, in which case, there is no cap to the number of raises that can be made.

NO-LIMIT

In no-limit cash games and tournaments, there is typically no cap to the number of raises allowed, though there are cardrooms that still impose the three- or four-raise rule. There is also no limit to how high a bet or raise can be. Players may raise as often as they like and for all their chips.

The minimum bet in no-limit must be at least the size of the big blind. Thus, if the big blind is $5, then the minimum allowed bet is $5. And raises must be at least equal to the size of the previous bet or raise in the round. For example, a $10 bet can be raised $30 more to make it $40 total. If a succeeding player reraises, he would have to make it at least $30 more—since that is the size of the last raise—for $70 total.

HOW TO BET

A bet is made by either pushing the chips in front of you—an action which speaks for itself—or by verbally calling out the play, and then pushing the chips in front of you. Simply announce, "I call," "I bet," "I raise," or whatever clearly indicates your desire, and then push your chips out on the felt. Note that if you announce a check, bet, raise, or a fold, it is binding and you're committed to the action.

Your bet should be placed at least six inches toward the middle, but not so far that your chips mingle with those already in the pot and cannot be distinguished from them. That is, your chips should be far enough away from your own stack and the pot so that they are clearly seen not only as a bet, but as your bet.

Do not throw your chips into the actual pot, which is called **splashing the pot**. This protects all players from an opponent intentionally or unintentionally miscalling a bet. Betting properly also allows the amount of the wager to easily be verified while making it clear to all players that a bet or raise has been made.

To check, tap or knock on the table with your fingertips or hand or announce "I check" or "check." To fold, push your cards or toss them face down towards the dealer. It is illegal to show your cards to active players who are competing for the pot.

BETTING ETIQUETTE

You should wait for your turn to play before announcing or revealing to any opponents what decision you will make. For example, if you know you're going to fold, you shouldn't toss your cards to the dealer before the action comes around to your position. And when you do give up your hand, pass the cards to the dealer face down, so that no other player can view them. If any cards are revealed to any one player, the rules of the game require that all players see them so that everyone is kept on equal footing.

It is improper and illegal to discuss your hand or another player's hand while a game is in progress. It is also very poor form to criticize other players' strategy decisions, no matter how poor they appear to be. If you think an opponent plays poorly, then that's good news for you: go win his chips.

THE BASICS OF POKER

TABLE STAKES, TAPPED OUT PLAYERS, AND SIDE POTS

You may only bet or call bets up to the amount of money you have on the table. This is called **table stakes**. You are not allowed to withdraw money from your wallet, borrow from other players, or receive credit while a hand is in progress. Getting extra cash or chips is permissible only before the cards are dealt.

For example, if the bet is $25 and you only have $10, you may only call for $10. The remaining $15 and all future monies bet during this hand—except for bets by opponents to equal the $10—would be separated into a **side pot**. A player who has no more table funds from which to bet is **tapped-out**.

A tapped-out player can still receive cards until the showdown and play for the **main pot**, however, he can no longer bet in this hand and has no interest in the side pot. The other active players can continue to bet against each other for the money in the side pot in addition to remaining in competition for the main pot with the tapped-out player.

At the showdown, if the tapped-out player has the best hand, he receives only the money in the main pot. The side pot will be won by the player having the best hand among the remaining players. Should one of the other players hold the overall best hand, that player wins both the original pot and the side pot.

If only one opponent remains when a player taps out, then there is no more betting, and cards are played out until the showdown, where the best hand wins.

SAMPLE ROUND OF BETTING

For illustrative purposes, let's follow the play in the first betting round of a private game of draw poker. The players have agreed to play with antes only and without any forced opening bets, so the first player to act may check or bet as desired. In the typical games we'll discuss later, in which a bet is due on the first round of betting, the first player to act has no such luxury. He must either call the blind or opening bring-in, or fold. In these games, checking is not possible in that first round.

The eight players have agreed to play $5/$10 limits with a $1 ante, so the pot holds $8 before any of the cards are dealt. Since this is the first round of betting, all bets and raises are in $5 increments. $10 bets and raises are not allowed in this round. Clockwise from the dealer, the participants are: Julian, Eddie-boy, Vicenzo, Fay, Donto, Flavian, Uncle J., and Big Phil (the current dealer).

They are playing **dealer's choice**, an option which allows each successive dealer to choose the variation played during his deal. In casino poker games, dealer's choice is not played, and players are limited to playing the variations designated for their table. If a player wishes to play a different variation, he must switch to a table offering the game he desires.

But in this home game, Big Phil is the current dealer, and he has chosen draw poker. He finishes shuffling the cards and deals out five cards to each player.

Julian, who sits on Big Phil's immediate left, goes first. He raps on the table with his knuckles. This is a non-verbal signal used in poker to indicate a check. He may also indicate his decision by saying "Check" or any verbal communication that would make this decision clear to the other players. Eddie-boy and Vicenzo, in turn, check as well. Play passes on to Fay, the next player.

Fay announces, "I'll bet $5," and pushes a $5 chip in front of her. Now that a bet is placed, no player can check and remain in the game. It will cost at least $5 to play.

Donto, sitting at Fay's left, decides his hand isn't worth $5. He flips his cards face down toward the dealer. Donto is no longer a participant in the pot, and he forfeits his $1 ante. He must wait until the next deal to resume play.

Flavian draws a big puff out of his cigar. "Cuban," he claims, and throws $10 into the pot, calling Fay's $5 bet and raising it $5 more. He announces, "$10 to you, Uncle J."

Raises, like bets, are made by placing chips in the area in front of the player. In a private game, players often toss the chips directly into the pot, however, in a casino game, these bets should be placed in front of the player so they don't commingle with the chips already in the pot. It is often the custom in a private game to announce them as well. Raising may be indicated by saying, "I'll raise you," "I'll call that bet and raise," or any such communication that clearly indicates that a raise is being made. In a cardroom, the simple placement of chips in front of your position is all that is needed to indicate that a bet or raise has been made.

Uncle J. must be daunted by the $10 he's due to play, or the cigar, and he folds. Big Phil, the dealer for this round of play, calls the $5 bet and the $5 raise, and reraises $5 more by placing $15 into the pot.

Flavian's cigar whirls across his mouth like a brigate cannon searching out new targets, and sends the long overdue ashes crashing against the dizzying colors of his Hawaiian short-sleeved shirt. One ash, still hot, works its way into a palm tree, and then fades away in lasting glory.

Play now returns to Julian, who had checked earlier. To stay in the hand, he must call $15 worth of bets—one $5 bet plus two $5 raises. He throws his cards in without hesitation, and is followed by Eddie-boy, who does the same. Vicenzo, who had also checked, calls the $15.

Fay plays next, and she must call the two $5 raises of her original bet to stay in active competition for the pot. She might have called just one raise, but with two raises facing her and Flavian's cigar bent at a mean angle, she decides her hand is not worth $10 more. She folds. She's out her earlier $5 bet and $1 ante—that money belongs to the pot.

Play passes by Donto, since he folded earlier, and proceeds to Flavian, the first raiser, and his cigar. Since his raise had been upped $5 by Big Phil, he must call that reraise to play. The cigar rotates slowly as Flavian weighs the possibility of raising again, and then pointedly stops, aimed dead ahead at the middle of Big Phil's forehead. Another second passes, drawn out by a long puff, and then Flavian flips a $5 chip into the pot, calling Big Phil's raise.

The only remaining players are, in order, Big Phil, Vicenzo, and Flavian. Big Phil cannot raise again. He was the last player to raise, and a player cannot raise his own bet. Since all bets and raises have been called by the remaining players, the betting round is over.

Though we used draw poker as an example, the same procedures apply to all forms of poker. Betting proceeds clockwise and every player gets a turn to bet. The round ends when no more bets or raises have been left unanswered.

THE RAKE

One of the biggest difference between casino poker and private poker games is that in casino games the house gets a cut of the action, called a **rake**, as its fee for hosting the game. In low-limit games and online, the rake can be anywhere from 5% to 10%, usually with a cap of $3 to $5 per pot. In higher limit games, the house typically charges players by time.

Time collection, where the house charges players by the half-hour or hour, is the preferred method of rakes. Typically, this will come out to a smaller fee than rakes taken directly out of the pot. While you generally don't have a choice given that you'll be playing where you'll be playing, you should be aware of the size rake that a cardroom collects, as it greatly impacts your profit potential. In a sense, the rake is a "tax." Obviously, the lower the rake, the better it is for your bottom line.

In tournaments, the house rake is collected up front. For example, a tournament with a $500 entry fee may add $40 to the $500 so your real cost might be $540. The $500 goes into the prize pool for the players, while the $40 goes to the dealers as a tip and the house for its fee.

The rake is a very real cost of playing and will eat into your profits. For example, if you're playing dead-even poker against the other players, you will end up a loser because of the money you lose to the house through the rake. To show a profit in cardroom poker, you need to not only beat the other players, but earn enough profits to cover the cost of the rake. If a group of players play long a rake game long enough, eventually, the house will have all the money!

THE RULES OF THE TABLE

Though poker is basically the same game played any-where, at home or in a cardroom, rules and procedures can vary from game to game. Make sure that you're clear about the particulars of play before sitting down at a new poker game. The most important questions to ask are:

1. What are the betting limits?
2. Are antes or blinds used, and if so, how much are they?
3. What is the maximum number of raises al-lowed?

When you're playing in a cardroom, you can ask the dealer or a player and add a fourth question: "How much is the rake?" And in a private game, "Is check-and-raise allowed?"

In a tournament, a player's hand can be ruled dead if he is not physically in his seat and his cards will be taken away. Sometimes, the tournament rules state that the hand is dead when the dealer begins dealing. Other times, it might be when the last card has been dealt or the absent player's turn is up. You'll want to be aware of the official rules so you don't lose out on any hands.

5. TEXAS HOLD'EM

Texas hold'em, or **hold'em**, as the game is more commonly known, is played as high poker, that is, the player with the best and highest five-card combination at the showdown wins the money in the pot. The pot can also be won by a player when all of his opponents fold their hands at any point before the showdown, leaving one player alone to claim the chips in the middle—even though he may not have held the best hand!

Your final five-card hand in hold'em will be made up of the best five-card combination of the seven total cards available to you. These include the **board**, five cards dealt face-up in the middle of the table which are shared by all players, and your **pocket cards** or **hole cards**, two cards dealt face-down that can be used by you alone. For example, your final hand could be composed of your two pocket cards and three cards from the board, one pocket card and four from the board, or simply all five board cards.

At the beginning of a hand, each player is dealt two face-down cards. Then each player gets a chance to exercise his betting options. Next, three cards are dealt simultaneously on the table for all players to share.

This is called the **flop**, and it is followed by another round of betting. A fourth board card, called the **turn**, is then dealt, and it too is followed by a round of betting. One final community card is dealt in the center of the table, making five total. This is the **river**. If two or more players remain in the hand, it is followed by the fourth and final betting round.

When all betting has finished, there is the **showdown**, in which the highest ranking hand in play wins.

HOW TO READ YOUR HOLD'EM HAND

You have all seven cards available to form your final five-card hand—any combination of your two hole cards and the five cards from the board. You can even use all five board cards. Let's look at an example.

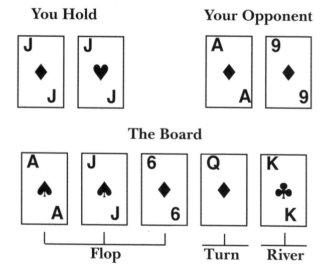

Your best hand, three jacks, is made using your two pocket cards and one jack from the board. This beats your opponent's pair of aces, formed with one card from his hand and one from the board. In both instances, the other cards are not relevant. For example, there is no need to say three jacks with an ace and a king versus two aces with a king, queen and jack—simply, three jacks versus two aces.

If the river card, the last card turned up on the board, had been a K♦ instead of a K♣, your opponent would have a diamond flush (formed with his two pocket diamonds and the three diamonds on the board), which would beat your set of jacks.

THE PLAY OF THE GAME

All play and strategy in hold'em depends upon the position of the **button**, which is a small disk, typically plastic and labeled "Dealer." The player who has the button in front of him, who is also known as the button, will have the advantage of acting last in every round of betting except for the preflop round. After each hand is completed, the disk rotates clockwise to the next player.

The two players to the left of the button are required to post bets, called **blinds**, before the cards are dealt. The player immediately to the button's left is called the **small blind** and the one to his left is called the **big blind**.

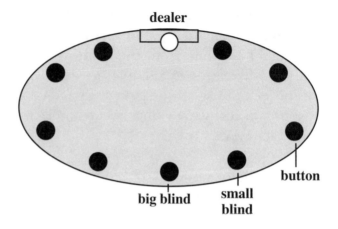

The big blind is typically the same size as the lower bet in a limit structure, so if you're in a $3/$6 game, the big blind would be $3 and in a $5/$10 game, it would be $5. The small blind will either be half the big blind in games where the big blind evenly divides to a whole dollar, or two-thirds of the big blind when it doesn't. For example, the small blind might be $2 in a $3/$6 game and $10 in a $15/$30 game.

Typical blinds for no-limit cash games might be $2/$5, $3/$5 or $5/$10 for the small blind and big blind respectively. Bigger blinds mean more action and larger games.

In cash games, the amount of the blinds are preset and remain constant throughout the game. In tournaments, however, the blinds steadily increase as the event progresses, forcing players to play boldly to keep up with the greater costs of the forced bets.

ORDER OF BETTING

Play always proceeds clockwise around the table. On the preflop, the first betting round, the first player to the left of the big blind goes first. He can call the big blind to stay in competition for the pot, raise, or fold. Every player following him has the same choices: call, raise, or fold. The last player to act on the preflop is the big blind. If no raises have preceded his turn, the big blind can either end the betting in the round by calling, or he can put in a raise.

However, if there are any raises in the round, the big blind and other remaining players must call or raise these bets to stay active, or they must fold.

On the other betting rounds—the flop, turn and river—the first active player to the button's left will go first and the player on the button will go last. If the button has folded, the player sitting closest to his right will act last. When all bets and raises have been met on the flop and turn, or if all players check, then the next card will be dealt. On the river, after all betting action is completed, players will reveal their cards to see who has the best hand.

Betting in a round stops when the last bet or raise has been called and no bets or raises are due any player. Players cannot raise their own bets or raises.

At any time before the showdown, if all opponents fold, then the last active player wins the pot.

> **Playing Tip**
> Never fold the big blind unless the pot has been raised. If there is no raise, there is no cost to play and you can see the flop for free.

SAMPLE GAME

Let's follow the action in a sample $3/$6 limit game with nine players so that you can see how hold'em is played.

In limit poker, the betting structure has two levels, the lower levels being the amount you must bet or raise on the preflop and flop ($3 in a $3/$6 game), and the higher levels being the amount you must bet or raise on the turn and river ($6 in a $3/$6 game).

Before the cards are dealt, the small blind and the big blind must post their bets. Once that occurs, the dealer will distribute cards one at a time, beginning with the small blind, who is the player sitting to the immediate left of the button, and proceeding clockwise until all players have received two face down cards.

The Preflop

The player to the big blind's left acts first. He has the option of calling the $3 big blind bet, raising it $3 more, or folding. Checking is not an option on the preflop as there is already a bet on the table—the $3 big blind bet.

Let's say this player folds. The next player is faced with the same decisions: call, raise, or fold. He calls for $3. Since this is a $3/$6 game, all bets and raises in this round must be in $3 increments. The next three players fold. The following player raises $3, making it $6 total—the $3 call plus the $3 raise.

It is the button's turn, the player sitting in the dealer position. He thinks about his cards and calls the $6. Now it is up to the small blind. The small blind has already put in $2 so he must put in $4 more to play. If there had been no raise, it would cost him just $1 more to meet the $3 big blind bet and stay active.

The small blind folds and the big blind considers reraising the raiser, but instead just calls the $3 raise. Play now moves back to the original caller. Since he has only put $3 into the pot, he must meet the $3 raise to stay in the hand. He calls and since all bets and raises have been matched, the round is over. We'll see the flop four-handed.

The big blind always has the option to raise on the preflop. The dealer will announce, "Option," on the big blind's turn alerting him to this. If there had been no raises and the big blind calls, the betting is finished for the round. If the big blind raises, then the other active players must meet that raise to stay active.

If all players fold on the preflop, the big blind wins the hand by default.

The Flop

At the conclusion of betting, the dealer pulls the blinds and bets into the pot. He takes the top card off the deck and **burns** it, that is, he removes it from play, and then deals the three card flop face-up in the center of the table.

Bets and raises during this round are still at the $3 level. The first active player to the button's left goes first. Since the small blind has folded, it is the big blind's turn. There are no bets that have to be met—the forced first round blind bet only occurs on the preflop—so the big blind may check or bet. (There is no reason to fold, which would be foolish, as it costs nothing to stay active.)

The big blind checks, the next player checks, the original raiser from the preflop checks, and it is now up to the button. He pushes $3 into the pot forcing the other three players to put up $3 if they want to see another card. The big blind, who checked first in this round, is the next active player. He must call or raise this bet to continue with the hand, or he must fold. He decides to call for $3 and the other two players fold. Since all bets have been called, betting is complete for the round.

We're now heads-up, the big blind versus the button.

The Turn

The dealer burns the top card and then deals a fourth community card face-up on the table. This is known as the **turn** or **fourth street**. Betting moves to the upper limit, so now all bets and raises are in $6 increments. The big blind, being the first active player on the button's left, goes first and checks. The button checks as well. Since all active players checked, the betting round is over.

The River and the Showdown

After the top card is burned, the fifth and final community card is turned over and placed next to the other four cards in the center of the table. Players now have five community cards along with their two pocket cards to form their final five-card hand.

At the **river** or **fifth street**, which this round is called, there is one final round of betting. The big blind goes first and leads out with a $6 bet. The button calls, and that concludes the betting since the big blind cannot raise his own bet. We now have the showdown. The big blind turns over K-Q, which combines with a board of K-Q-10-7-5 for two pair of kings and queens. The button's K-10 also gives him two pair led by kings, but his second pair is tens. The big blind has the superior hand and wins the money in the pot.

Had the button simply folded, the big blind would have won by default, since no other players remained to contest the pot.

On the showdown, the last player to bet or raise (or if there has been no betting in the round, then the first person to the left of the button) has to show his cards first. Losers can simply **muck** their cards, that is, fold them, without showing their cards.

The dealer pushes the chips in the pot over to the winner, collects and shuffles the cards, and prepares to deal a new hand. The button moves clockwise, so the big blind is now the small blind, and the small blind becomes the button.

6. HOLD'EM'S SEVEN KEY STRATEGIC CONCEPTS

The following key concepts apply to all forms of hold'em.

1. RESPECT POSITION

In hold'em, where you sit relative to the button is called **position**. In a nine-handed game, the first three spots to the left of the button are known as **early position**, the next three, **middle position**, and the last three, **late position**. In a ten-handed game, early position is the four spots to the left of the button.

The later the position, the bigger the advantage, because you get to see what your opponents do before deciding whether to commit any chips to the pot. The earlier the position, the more vulnerable your hand is to being raised and thus the more powerful your hand must be for you to enter the pot.

In late position, you have more options and leverage so you can play more hands. If the early betting action is aggressive, you can fold marginal hands without cost. And if the betting action is weak, you can be more aggressive with marginal hands and see the flop with better position.

2. PLAY GOOD STARTING CARDS

You must start out with good cards to give yourself the best chance to win. And while this seems obvious, you'd be surprised at the number of players who ignore this basic strategic concept and take loss after loss by chasing with inferior and losing hands. If you play too many hands in poker, you'll soon find yourself without chips. Enter the pot with good starting cards in the right position and you give yourself good chances to finish with winners.

3. PLAY OPPONENTS

By watching how an opponent plays, you get all sorts of information on how to take advantage of his tendencies. For example, when a player infrequently enters a pot, he's **tight**, and you can often force him out of hands even when he may have better cards than you. You'll give him credit for big hands when he's in a pot, and get out of his way unless you have a big hand yourself.

On the other hand, an opponent who plays a lot of hands is **loose**, and you can figure him for weaker cards on average. You also need to adjust for **aggressive** players, who often raise when they get involved in a pot, and **passive** players, opponents you can play against with less fear of getting raised.

4. BE THE AGGRESSOR

Hold'em is a game where aggression brings the best returns. It's almost always better to raise than to call. Raising immediately puts pressure on opponents who will often fold right there, unwilling to commit chips to their marginal hands. Or they will see the flop but will be ready to drop out against further bets if it doesn't connect strongly enough with their cards—which happens most of the time.

5. WIN CHIPS, NOT POTS

You want to win chips and to do so, you need to win pots, particularly big ones if you can. So keep this in mind: It is not the quantity of pots you win, but the quality of them that matters.

6. FOLD LOSING HANDS

Part of winning is minimizing losses when you have the second best hand. This means not chasing pots when you are a big underdog to win, especially longshot draws against heavy betting. You can't win them all. Save your chips for better opportunities. Cutting losses on hands you lose adds to overall profits.

7. PATIENCE

Hold'em is a game of patience. You will often go long stretches between good hands. Winning players exercise patience and wait for situations where they can win chips. Your good hands will come, and if you haven't blown yourself out trying to force plays, you'll be able to take advantage of them and win some nice pots for yourself.

7. LIMIT HOLD'EM STRATEGY

In limit hold'em, where all betting is in a two-tier structure, such as $3/$6 or $5/$10, the three main factors to consider when deciding how to play a hand are the strength of your starting cards, where you are sitting relative to the button, and the action that precedes your play.

There are other considerations that enter into the mix, such as the cost of entering the pot and the aggressiveness or tightness of the table, but you should always consider these three fundamental factors first.

STARTING CARDS

The biggest mistake novices and habitually losing players make in hold'em is playing too many hands. Each call costs at least one bet. They compound this mistake when they catch a piece of the flop—but not enough of it—leading to more inadvisable bets and raises when they are holding a losing hand, thus making the situation even more costly. These lost chips add up quickly and set the stage for losing sessions.

So the foundation of playing winning hold'em is starting with solid cards, that is, playing the right cards in the right positions.

We'll divide the starting hands into four different categories: Premium, Playable, Marginal, and Junk.

PREMIUM STARTING HANDS

A-A   K-K   A-K   Q-Q   J-J

Limit hold'em is a game of big cards. Aces, kings, queens, jacks, and A-K are the best starting hands. They are strong enough to raise from any position at the table and should be played aggressively. You hope to accomplish two things with the raise. First, you want to get more money into the pot on a hand in which you're probably leading, and second, you want to protect that hand by narrowing the field of opponents. The greater the number of players who stay in the pot, the greater the chances that a weaker hand will draw out and beat your premium hand.

If a player raises ahead of you or reraises behind you, reraise with aces and kings, and just call with the other premium hands and see how the flop goes. Jacks are weaker than the other big pairs because there is about a 50% chance that an overcard, a queen, king, or ace will come on the flop, making your hand vulnerable to players holding hands such as A-K, A-Q, and K-Q, or really, ace-any—an ace with any other card.

If an overcard flops when you have jacks, queens, or even kings, or you miss entirely with A-K, you have to think about giving up on these hands if an opponent bets into you or check-raises. For example, if the flop is Q-7-6 and you have A-K or J-J, and an opponent leads into you, you're probably donating chips. A better flop would be K-10-3 for A-K or 10-8-2 for J-J.

It's also tough to play high pairs against an ace flop since players will often play starting cards containing an ace. And in low-limit games, you'll get players seeing the flop with all sorts of hands, so if there are a bunch of players in the pot, you have to be concerned about an ace flopping when you have a big pocket pair, such as kings. If you have A-K, however, that flop puts you in a strong position, especially in a game where opponents like to play ace-anything.

You're also concerned with flops of three connecting cards, such as 8-9-10 and three suited cards if you don't have the ace of the same suit for a powerful **flush draw**—four cards of one suit needing one more card of that suit to complete a flush. These are not good flops for big pairs or an A-K.

PLAYABLE STARTING HANDS

A-Q   A-J   A-10   K-Q   10-10   9-9   8-8

These starting hands should be folded in early position. They should also be folded in middle or late position if the pot has been raised from early position, which suggests strength, unless you think the raiser is loose and you can see the flop for just that one bet.

If players **limp** into the pot before you—that is, if they just call the bet—you can limp in as well with the playable hands. Sometimes a raise will be good if you can force out players behind you and isolate the limper. However, if you're in there against loose players who are not easily moved off a pot, which will generally be the case in low limit poker games, you might consider calling. When you're up against opponents who cannot be chased by raises, you'd prefer to see the flop for one bet with these hands.

If you enter the pot and it gets raised after you, you have to make a decision. If the raise comes from late position and it's from a loose player, you have more reason to call then to fold. It's just one bet. However, if it's raised twice and costs you two more bets, or it looks like you might be trapped between a bettor and a raiser, get away from these hands while it's still cheap. There is too much strength against you.

What if no one has entered the pot before you? If you're in middle or late position, you should raise coming into the pot and try to limit the field or even better, get the blinds.

MARGINAL STARTING HANDS

7-7   6-6   5-5   4-4   3-3   2-2
K-J   Q-J   K-J   Q-10   K-10   J-10
A-x (ace with any other card)
Suited connectors: 5-6, 6-7, 7-8, 8-9, 9-10

Play marginal hands only if you can get in for one bet—but not at the cost of two bets. This means you'll fold these hands in early and middle position where you are vulnerable to being raised.

In late position, call in an unraised pot, but if the pot has already been raised from early or middle position or you are between a bettor and a raiser, these marginal cards become unprofitable and should be folded.

If there is a raise after you enter the pot, you can call with these marginal hands—when the cost is only one bet—but fold in the face of a double raise or in situations where yet another raise can follow.

PLAYING LATE POSITION

You can play many more hands from late position. You've had a chance to see the betting before it reaches your position. If the action is heavy, you fold all non-premium hands. If the action is light and the cost is cheap, you can get more creative. And if no one has entered the pot, you should often raise, as there is a good chance no one will call and you'll get the blinds.

If there are only limpers, you add **suited connectors**—hands that are consecutive in rank, such as 5-6 or 8-9 and in the same suit—to your starting hands. Suited connectors are best played in a pot with three or more players. You want multiple opponents in the pot so that you can win a bunch of chips if you hit your hand. If the pot is raised and it would cost you two bets to play, call only if it looks like there will be enough players in to see the flop.

Pairs of twos through sevens are played similarly to connectors preflop. You want to play them in late position when you can see the flop cheaply and get a multiway pot. If there are several callers, you should call, but if the pot has been raised, meaning it will now cost you two bets to play, you can quietly muck the small pair. If you've already bet and the pot gets raised, you can call that extra bet as long as you feel that you won't get trapped and raised again.

Though a pair will only improve to a three of a kind hand about one time in eight, when it does, you'll be sitting with a big hand that can trap opponents for a lot of chips. If it doesn't improve and there are overcards on the flop, you probably have the worst of it and should fold against an opponent's bet. One rule of thumb here—no set, no bet.

JUNK HANDS

All other hands not shown in the above three categories should be folded. They are heavy underdogs with little chance of winning. If you're in the big blind and the pot is unraised, by all means take the flop for free. But if it costs you to see the flop, fold immediately. It's cheaper watching this round as a bystander.

OTHER CONSIDERATIONS

If you miss the flop and think that betting will cause your opponent to fold, make the play. Otherwise, don't throw chips at longshots. Save them for better spots.

Be careful playing flush and straight draws unless they're to the **nuts**—the best hand possible given the cards on board. For example, you don't want to play a straight draw if there is a flush draw on board, or if you have, say, the 6-7 on a board of 7-8-9-10-X. Any opponent with a jack will bust you here. And given that many players like to play J-10, that 7-8-9 flop is dangerous to your hand.

HOLD'EM PREFLOP MATCHUPS
(NO CARDS SHARE SUITS UNLESS SPECIFIED)

HAND MATCHUP	HAND A WIN %	HAND B WIN %	TIE %
Pair vs. Pair			
A-A vs. K-K	80.79%	18.81%	.40%
A-A vs. 6-6	79.44%	20.26%	.30%
Aces vs. Ace-King			
A-A vs. A-K	91.98%	6.80%	1.22%
A-A vs. A-K suited	87.26%	11.47%	1.27%
Aces vs. Connectors			
A-A vs. J-10	81.98%	17.68%	.34%
A-A vs. J-10 suited	78.34%	21.28%	.38%
A-A vs. 6-5	81.07%	18.65%	.28%
A-A vs. 6-5 suited	76.56%	23.07%	.38%
Pair vs. Two Overcards			
10-10 vs. A-K	56.66%	43.04%	.30%
10-10 vs. A-K suited	53.84%	45.81%	.34%
6-6 vs. A-K	55.34%	44.32%	.34%
6-6 vs. A-K suited	52.23%	47.42%	.35%
2-2 vs. J-10	50.82%	47.72%	1.46%
2-2 vs. J-10 suited	53.05%	45.54%	1.41%
Pair vs. One Overcard (Dominated)			
K-K vs. A-K	69.70%	29.45%	.85%
K-K vs. A-K suited	65.16%	34.00%	.84%
6-6 vs. 7-6	62.74%	34.42%	2.84%
6-6 vs. 7-6 suited	59.22%	37.91%	2.86%
Pair vs. One Overcard			
K-K vs. A-Q	71.62%	28.08%	.30%
K-K vs. A-Q suited	67.48%	32.17%	.35%
10-10 vs. A-2	71.33%	28.24%	.44%
10-10 vs. A-2 suited	67.25%	32.36%	.40%
6-6 vs. A-2	69.68%	29.87%	.44%
6-6 vs. A-2 suited	65.88%	33.66%	.46%
Dominated Hands			
A-K vs. A-Q	71.80%	23.71%	4.49%
A-K vs. A-Q suited	67.15%	28.30%	4.55%
A-K vs. A-6	71.27%	24.41%	4.32%

8. NO-LIMIT HOLD'EM STRATEGY

In no-limit hold'em, your entire stack of chips is at risk on every single hand—as are those of your opponents. One big mistake and they're gone. In limit hold'em, one bet is only one bet. In no-limit, that one bet could be the defining moment of your game because it could be for all your chips. And that changes the way you play hands.

No-limit hold'em appears deceptively simple at first glance, but as you get deeper into the strategies and the situations that occur, you start to see the many complexities of the game.

STARTING HANDS

If you're the first player coming into the pot on the preflop, you generally want to enter the pot with a **standard raise**, three times the size of the big blind. So if the big blind is at $5, make your raise $15, and if it's $10, make your raise $30.

The reason you don't make the raise two times the big blind is that you make it too easy for your opponents, particularly the big blind, to enter the pot cheaply with marginal hands, subjecting your hand to lucky draws from opponents who might not otherwise see the flop.

You want your preflop raises to consistently be three times the size of the big blind so that opponents get no extra information on the strength of your hand. Players that vary their preflop raises are sometimes announcing their hands. And if your opponents limp in to see the flop and you have a raising hand, make it four times the big blind. There is now more money in the pot and you want to make it unprofitable for them to call with marginal cards.

The hammer of the big bet or the all-in bet in no-limit hold'em puts a lot of pressure on opponents who hold marginal hands as well as strong hands in which they don't have confidence. Even when opponents think you're bluffing, it costs chips for them to find out for sure, which is often a greater cost than they're willing to risk.

THE PREFLOP: EARLY POSITION
The best starting cards in no-limit hold'em are the **premium hands**—pocket aces, kings, queens, jacks, A-K, and A-Q. In an unraised pot, bring these hands in for a standard raise in early position. Your goal is to narrow the field to one or two callers and to either win the pot right there when all players fold or reduce the number of players who will see the flop.

If you have aces or kings, hopefully you'll get a caller or two, or even better, a raiser. Then you'll raise right back the size of the pot or go in for all your chips if you get reraised. With queens and A-K, you can stand a raise to see the flop, but if the raise is for all your chips and you're not short-stacked, you may need to let these hands go. If you don't want your day finished with queens, you certainly don't want to go out on jacks or A-Q! If an opponent goes all-in when you hold J-J or A-Q, or even puts in a big raise, these are grounds for folding these hands.

If a player comes in raising before you, the aces and kings are automatic reraises and the non-premium hands are automatic folds. Lean towards calling with A-K and queens. If the raiser is tight, fold with A-Q and jacks; if the raiser is loose, raising or calling are both viable options. Remember, no play is set in stone in no-limit hold'em. You need to judge hands on a situation by situation basis.

Pass on all other hands from early position, especially against an aggressive table. If the table is tight, or it's early in a tournament and there's little cost to enter the pot, you may take a flier on a hand now and then to mix it up.

MIDDLE POSITION

In middle position, you can play more hands due to the simple fact that you have fewer players behind who can raise your bets. If there is a raise before your turn, consider folding all non-premium hands. You don't want to go into the flop as a big underdog, which this earlier position raise probably indicates. And if the raiser is tight, fold jacks and A-Q as well. If you have aces or kings, reraise and have no fear of getting all your chips in the middle. You can also reraise with queens and A-K, or you could just call.

If no one has raised in front of you, you will still play the premium hands for a raise and can add the second tier hands—eights, nines and tens, along with A-J, A-10, and K-Q to your list of raising hands. If you get reraised by a player behind you, consider throwing second tier hands away. These hands have value, but against heavy betting, they're chip burners.

Of course, if your opponent is low on chips and moves in on the preflop, especially in a tournament, give him credit for holding lesser quality cards and be prepared to play all premium hands—but again, use judgment. When in doubt, go with your gut feeling.

LATE POSITION

In late position, if the pot has been raised in early position, reraise with A-A, K-K, Q-Q and A-K. If you get reraised, you may consider just calling with Q-Q and A-K, and if the raiser is tight and goes all-in, you probably want to release these hands. And you certainly do not want to be in that reraised pot with jacks, A-Q or anything less. With aces and kings, you're always ready to play for all the marbles preflop.

If the pot is raised in middle position, reraise with the top four hands, A-A, K-K, Q-Q, and A-K. How you play jacks and A-Q is a judgment call, but it may be safer just to call and see the flop.

If there has been no raiser in the pot, you can expand your starting hands to any pair, an ace with any other card, and any two cards 10 or higher, for example, Q-10 or K-J. Generally, it's best to come in raising. Most of the time, you'll win the blinds, which is good. If you get callers, you have some value to see the flop.

If you get aces or kings in late position and you think you'll get a caller, raise. If not, it might be better to limp in. You don't get kings or aces often, but when you do, you want to make money on them.

You can also play suited connectors, such as 6-7, 7-8, 8-9, and 10-J, if you can see the flop cheaply.

THE BLINDS

The blinds have the advantage of going last in the first round of play but the big disadvantage of going first in all other rounds. Play the blinds according to the advice in the early position strategy section.

If a late position bettor continually raises you out of the pot when you're the big blind, then you have to take a stand at some point to keep that opponent in line. You'd like to have two big cards or ace-anything to reraise with, but you can also do this with garbage.

If you read him correctly, he'll fold and you've got his chips. Do this once or twice and you'll get his attention and respect.

If everyone folds to you in the small blind and you can see the flop cheaply, it's not a bad play to call the big blind. You may flop something pretty or check to the showdown and win with better garbage than your opponent.

If there is no raise and you're in the big blind, and you're not in a raising situation, always see it for free— don't make the mistake of folding!

THE FLOP

If you came in raising preflop, you want to continue playing aggressively. If you're first, bet regardless of what flops. Your opponent will probably fold and you've got the pot. If he calls and you don't improve, you might consider checking on the turn. If he raises you, it's a tough call, but you'll have to consider giving up the hand unless you feel you've got better. Now, if you're second, and he checks, bet out at him.

What if he bets into you? If you miss the flop, give him the pot. Since you've shown strength preflop, his bet on the flop means you're probably second-best.

When you have what you think is the best hand, your goal is to take the pot immediately, particularly when there are straight and flush draws possible, for example, two cards of the same suit are on the board. You don't want opponents playing for another card cheaply, making it, and then destroying you on a hand that shouldn't have even seen another card. If opponents are going to beat you, make them pay to do so.

However, if you have an absolute monster like a full house or quads, you want to keep players in and extract more bets out of them. Often, that means checking and hoping a free card gives them a bigger hand.

THE TURN
If you've played aggressively on the preflop and flop, and your opponent hasn't budged, you have to figure him for possible strength. It's time for you to look at what you think he thinks you have. If you're representing strength and playing tight, you have to give him credit for a strong hand and slow down your betting. If he checks, you check, and if you're first, check to him and see how he reacts.

THE RIVER
When you have a big hand that you're confident is the best, you want to get more chips into the pot. If you're last and there have been no bets, put the amount of chips in the pot you feel your opponent will call. If you're first, you have two options: check or bet. If your opponent is very aggressive or has been leading at the pot, you can consider checking and letting him bet, then going over the top of him with a raise to try and get more chips in the pot. You want to be careful

not to move an opponent off a pot with a bet. Let your knowledge of how your opponent plays guide you.

When you have a strong hand but have doubts whether it's the best one out there, it's often better to check at the river, rather than bet and risk a big raise that you won't call. If your opponent checks, you'll see the showdown with no further cost. If he bets, you see what you want to do. Be careful about betting in an attempt to get an opponent to fold. He might raise you back or set you all in, and you'll be forced to muck your cards and give up your chips.

If you're going to bluff at the river, however, make sure it's for enough chips so that your opponent will be faced with a tough decision on whether to call.

CASH GAME STRATEGY

In cash games, you're not worried about blinds, because they're generally small, nor are you concerned with antes, because there aren't any. Your goal in a cash game is purely and simply to win chips. You don't care if you have more chips than other players, or less, as long as you finish playing with more of them than you started with. And then you have won money.

When you have a good session and win lots of chips, you can take them off the table and leave any time you want. The chips you play with can be converted to real profits at any time.

9. NO-LIMIT TOURNAMENT STRATEGY

In a tournament, your strategy boils down to one thing: survival. Your goal is to hang in there and move up the ladder as players get eliminated so that you can get into the prize money. And finally, you want to get to the final table or be the champion.

In a tournament, chips are power. If you have a lot of them, take advantage of your superior chip count by bullying short stacks and timid players with aggressive betting and by stealing their blinds. Anytime you bet and compete against a smaller stack, he knows that if he goes to war with you for all his chips and loses, he's eliminated. It is difficult for short stacks to play back at you because you can break them. Conversely, when you're that smaller stack, you must tread carefully against bigger stacks because your tournament will be at stake if all the chips go in the middle.

If you get **low-stacked**—that is, your chip stack is less than five times the size of the big blind—then you need to make a play for all your chips at the very first opportunity. If the pot is unraised and you have an ace with any other card, two cards 10 or higher, or any pair, go all-in and hope for the best. You cannot afford to play passive here—calling is not an option—you need the blinds and antes to stay alive.

Ideally, you would like your stack size to be at least ten times the size of the big blind. Either you take risks or you will get **blinded out**—lose all or a majority of your chips to the gradual forced blind and ante bets by barely playing any hands!

The most fundamental no-limit play to get chips is to steal the blinds. This is when you raise in late position when no one else has entered the pot so that opponents will fold and you can win the blinds without a fight. The best position to do this from is the button or the seat before the button. Often, the blinds will fold, giving you the pot uncontested. You don't want to make this play every time, because your opponents will catch on, but at the same time, if the blinds are going to give you the pot without a fight, well then, take it every time.

In all situations, if an opponent is short-stacked, give him credit for much less of a hand than you would normally expect and don't be afraid to play all premium hands for all of your opponent's chips. You can also consider playing back at him with any pair or two high cards if you have a lot of chips and a loss here won't make you low-stacked. Just as you would play all sorts of hands when your stack is desperately low, so would your opponent, so you can open up here and call an all-in bet with less of a hand.

EARLY ROUND
TOURNAMENT STRATEGY

In the first few rounds of a tournament, the blinds are generally small, and the antes won't kick in until the third or fourth level. During these early rounds, there is little pressure on you to make any moves as the blinds won't make too much of a dent in your stack, at least not a critical dent. Your strategy here is to play conservatively, trying to win little pots when possible and avoiding big pots unless you're reasonably convinced that you have the winner. You don't want to risk your tournament on a foolish bluff.

Your goal is to increase your chips stack as the tournament progresses, hopefully to double up after three rounds.

MIDDLE ROUND
TOURNAMENT STRATEGY

The middle rounds of a tournament, around levels four to eight, is when players start getting eliminated at a more rapid pace. The blinds and antes are more expensive and this means you have to play more hands and take more chances.

If you're low-stacked, aggressive play and stealing blinds becomes more important to keep up with the costs of feeding blinds and antes into the pot. If you're big-stacked, you want to push around the weak players and small stacks and get more chips. You're looking to position yourself for the final table.

LATE ROUND TOURNAMENT STRATEGY

If you've lasted into the later rounds, you've either made it into the money or are getting real close. Now you look forward, hoping to get to the final table and the bigger money. You want to pick up your game here and play your best poker. Avoid facing off in big pots or all-ins against stacks that can take you out—unless you've got the goods—but as always in a tournament, keep pushing your weight around against players that can be bullied.

FINAL TABLE

If you get to the final table, you have a real shot at winning, but you still have to get through the last players. If you're among the big stacks, avoid going to war against another big stack that can bust you or make you one of the small stacks. Use your big stack to put pressure on smaller stacks struggling to stay alive.

If you're low-stacked, the blinds and antes are exerting tremendous pressure, leaving you with little choice but to find your best opportunity and then go after it for all your chips. Calling is not an option here.

Think before you make your moves, keeping in mind that every player eliminated means a big jump in prize money.

10. OMAHA

Omaha has a well deserved reputation for being a game for action players. Pot-sizes tend to get large as players liberally splash chips around the table, especially in the high-low variations, where multiway pots and frequent raising make the game very exciting. More and more players are making Omaha their game of choice.

Omaha high, which is also called **Omaha**, is a high poker game that is played exactly like hold'em, except for two things. First, players are dealt four cards to start with, as opposed to just two as in hold'em. The second—and this is the part that confuses new players—you must use exactly two of your pocket cards, no more, no less, and three from the board to form your final five-card hand. Not only is it easy for new players to get confused, even world class players have been known to misread their hands in Omaha.

For example, if you were dealt four aces in the hole, you wouldn't have quads because only two of the aces would count toward the final hand! The remaining three cards would have to come from the board.

Omaha is played with a button, which moves clockwise

around the table after each deal, as well as a small blind and a big blind. The deal starts with each player getting four downcards, called **pocket cards** or **hole cards**. The first betting round proceeds exactly as in hold'em, with the player to the left of the big blind acting first.

When the betting action has been completed on the preflop round, the **flop** of three community cards is turned face-up in the center of the table. This is followed by a round of betting. The **turn** and **river** are similarly dealt, each followed by a betting round. At the showdown, the highest hand wins the pot.

Because of the additional starting cards, it's possible to form many more hands than in hold'em, and thus on average, you need much better hands to win a pot. In Omaha, with the four starting cards, there are actually 64 starting hand combinations! Compare that to hold'em, where there is only one. When you start combining those hands with a flop, many more hands become possible. You'll be able to make stronger hands, but be careful—so will your opponents!

Omaha can also be played as high-low in a variation called **Omaha high-low 8-or-better** or simply, **Omaha 8-or-better**. In this version, the best low hand and best high hand split the pot. However, if no hand qualifies for low—has five unpaired cards of 8 or lower—the best high hand scoops (wins the entire pot).

Players can choose two different five-card combinations to make their final hands, one for the high hand and one for the low hand. The best high hand and best low hand can be held by the same player; if so, that player scoops.

HOW TO READ AN OMAHA HIGH-LOW HAND

Here is an example showing how a high and low hand is made in conjunction with the board. If you hold A-A-J-4 with a board of A-J-7-6-2, two aces from your pocket cards are used to form the high hand, A-A-A-J-7. The A and 4 would be combined with the 7-6-2 of the board to form a 7-6-4-2-A for low. Note that in both instances, two of your down cards and three community cards are used to make the final poker hand.

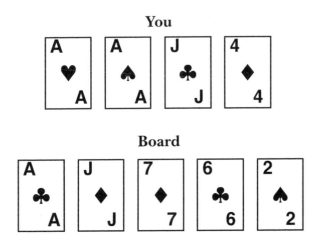

You

Board

Your Final High Hand

Your Final Low Hand

Note that you don't have a full house of aces over jacks for the high hand because, again, you can only use two of your hole cards. If your opponent holds 3-3-3-J, he would lose on the high end since he only has a pair of jacks! Since he must use his jack as part of the hand, he does not have a 7-6-3-2-A low, so he would lose on the low end as well.

Opponent

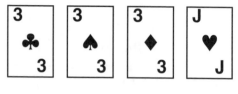

Opponent's Final High Hand

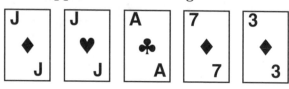

Opponent's Final Low Hand

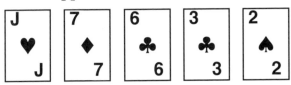

THE PLAY OF THE GAME

Omaha is played with a button, which moves clockwise around the table after each deal, as well as a small blind and a big blind. As in hold'em, position is extremely important in the Omaha games, since the button, or the player closest to the button's right, acts last in every round after the preflop.

The action starts with each player getting four hole cards. Then there is a betting round that starts with the player immediately to the left of the big blind. Since there is already a bet that needs to be met—the big blind—this first player must call or raise to stay active; otherwise he must fold.

In a limit betting structure, the big blind is normally equal to the lower bet, while the small blind is half that amount when the big blind is divisible by two. This is called either a two-and-four bet structure or a one-and-two chip structure. If the big blind isn't divisible by a whole number, then the small blind will be two-thirds of that amount. This would be a two-and-three chip blind structure.

For example, in a $3/$6 game, the big blind would be $3 and the small blind would be $2, and in a $15/$30 limit game, the big blind would be $15 and the small blind $10. In a $10/$20 game, the one-and-two chip structure would be used; here the big blind would be $10 and the small blind $5.

All bets in the first round must be in the lower increment: $3 in a $3/$6 game, $5 in a $5/$10 game, $15 in a $15/$30 game, and so on. If you were playing pot-limit, then you could bet up to the amount in the pot, and if no-limit were being played, your maximum bet would be limited only by the amount of chips you had on the table.

The action goes around the table until all bets and raises have been called. If all players fold to the big blind, he wins the pot by default. If players have called but not raised, the big blind can also call to end the betting for the round or exercise his option to raise and force opponents to match the raise if they want to remain in competition for the pot.

As in all poker games, action proceeds clockwise around the table. The first active player to the button's left always goes first and the button acts last, unless the button has folded, in which case the first active player to the button's right acts last. Unlike seven-card stud, where the order of betting changes depending upon the cards on board, in Omaha, position remains constant throughout a deal.

OMAHA

When the preflop betting action has been completed, three community cards are turned face-up in the center of the table. This is the flop, and it is followed by a second round of betting. In a limit betting structure, all bets on this round remain at the lower level of the two-tier structure. For example, in a $5/$10 game, all bets and raises would be for $5.

The first active player to the left of the button goes first. Since there are no forced bets this round or in the following rounds, he may open the action by checking or betting. (The first betting round, when the initial four cards are dealt, is the only time that players must put chips into the middle to stay active.) If all players check the flop, they'll all get to see the next card for free. However, if a bet is made by one of the players, his opponents must call that bet and any subsequent raises in order to stay in the hand.

If two or more players remain after the betting is completed, a fourth community card is dealt. This is the turn or **fourth street**. Another round of betting follows. Then comes the river or **fifth street**, in which a fifth community card is dealt face-up in the middle of the table. The river is the last card players will receive and it is followed by the last betting round.

In limit games, turn and river bets must be at the higher level of the betting structure. For example, $6 in a $3/$6 game, $10 in a $5/$10 game, and $30 in a $15/$30 game.

If two or more players remain after all betting has been completed, there is the showdown. Each player combines exactly two of his hole cards with three of the five community cards to form his best and final five-card hand. The highest ranking hand wins the showdown.

If at any time during the four betting rounds, one player has forced out all his opponents through bets and raises they wouldn't match, this player wins the pot by default. He collects all the antes, bets, and raises that were made.

OMAHA 8-OR-BETTER
GETTING QUARTERED AND SIXTHED

In Omaha high-low 8-or-better, players often split the pot at the showdown. In fact, there can be multiple split pots. For example, if two low hands are tied for best and there is a high-hand winner, the high hand will take half the pot, and the two low players will get **quartered**—meaning each of them will split the low half, getting just one quarter each of the total pot.

If there happens to be three low winners, they would split the low end three ways, getting one-sixth of the pot each, with the high winner taking sole possession of the high half of the pot. Ties for the best high hand would be divided the same way—all winners get an equal portion from the high half of the pot or from the whole pot if no player qualifies for low.

For there to be a winner on the low end, that hand must be no worse than five unpaired cards of 8 or better. For example, the hand 8-7-5-3-A qualifies for low, but the hand 8-7-5-2-2 does not because of the paired deuces. A hand of 9-7-3-2-A would not qualify either, even though it may be the lowest hand, because the 9-high hand doesn't meet the 8-or-better qualifier. In this case, the high-end winner or winners would get all the spoils.

STRATEGY FOR OMAHA HIGH-LOW 8-OR-BETTER

Omaha high-low 8-or-better is a free-wheeling game, and chips come in from all directions. With both a high pot and low pot to go after, many players stay interested in the pot, especially in low-limit "no fold'em" games, in which players will chase pots right to the river since the last card dealt can so dramatically change the complexion of a hand.

GENERAL STRATEGY

The first four cards dealt in Omaha—your hole cards—are the only cards you alone can use, so they play an important role in defining your chances of winning. As in all poker variations, you must start out with solid cards to give yourself the best chances of winning.

There are great starting cards, good starting cards, and poor starting cards, but what appears to be a good or bad preflop hand may change in a flash when the flop throws three more cards into the mix. And the final two community cards open up even more possibilities that could make or break your hand.

With such a wide range of possibilities, hopes stay high and betting can be fierce. Unlike hold'em, where the starting hand combinations are fewer and it is less common for more than two players to see the flop, in Omaha 8-or-better, multiple players often bet and raise liberally. This will get expensive if you play hands that aren't good enough to stand the action. Thus, you must play solid poker to survive Omaha 8-or-better with your chips intact. Don't get sucked into rampant betting unless your hand is worthy of all the action. In this game, speculation and loose play can lose you a bunch of chips in a hurry.

Omaha is a flop game, in which the button stays constant in a hand, so your position at the table is a major factor in how you play your cards and which hands you choose to see the flop with. Before we touch on these important points, the three key winning concepts of Omaha 8-or-better must be emphasized.

#1 Key Concept: Scooping
In high-low games of any type, there is one guiding principle that is the foundation of all winning strategies: play hands that have a chance to scoop the pot, that is, win both the high and low half of the pot. This is especially true in Omaha, particularly pot-limit versions.

#2 Key Concept: Aces

The best card in Omaha 8-or-better is the ace, and generally speaking, if you don't have one, you're better off not even being involved in the pot. The cost of playing to see the flop, turn, and river is too expensive in this game for you to get involved in pots without an ace. And while there are ace-less hands that have good potential to make you money, if you're a beginner, you can still play a profitable game without playing any of them.

The ace is so important in Omaha 8-or-better because it is the best low card and the best high card, and your goal is to scoop the pot. When you hold an ace, you have a chance to improve to the top pair, top two pair, top set, top straight, top flush and top full house as well. An ace is a boss card that gives you a big edge over any opponent who doesn't have one. And since most of the cards get dealt in a full-handed Omaha game, if you don't have an ace, you can count on one of your opponents having one and holding that boss-card advantage over you.

#3 Key Concept: Playing for the Nuts

With so many players seeing the flop and playing through to the river, it is important that you start out with hands that have the potential to be the **nuts**, the best hand possible given the cards on board. In other words, if you make a flush, it should be the best flush (one led by an ace), and if it's a straight, then you don't want the ignorant, or low, end of the straight. When you're going for low, your hand should have the potential to be the best possible low.

STARTING HAND REQUIREMENTS

You're dealt what you're dealt in Omaha 8-or-better, but if you had a choice, you'd rather have a low draw than a high draw for one very simple reason: a low hand can develop into a high hand (by forming a low straight, an ace-led nut flush, two pair, trips, full house, or quads) while still being the nut low. But a high hand can never develop into a low hand.

Three low cards give you a strong starting position in Omaha 8-or-better, so along with your ace, you'd like to have a 2 or a 3 and one more card 5 or below. You need the third low card because the three-card flop will often **duplicate** or **counterfeit** one of your good low cards, that is, pair it up, rendering it useless. For example, if you hold A-2-K-K, and the flop is 2-6-8, your 2 is counterfeited and useless to you since you must use two hole cards toward your low. You would need two more low cards that are not an ace or 2 to make a qualified low.

But if you held a third low card, say A-2-5-K, now your low draw contains four cards, since you'd use the A-5 from your hand toward a low. You only need one more non-pairing low card to be dealt to make your low hand. Thus, with a third low card, you stay very much in the hunt.

The best starters in Omaha 8-or-better have both high and low possibilities, so along with the ace plus 2 or 3 and third low card, you'd like another ace (A-A-3-5), or two suited cards, preferably led by the ace, so that you have a shot at a nut flush. A king is a good card to accompany the ace, for example A-2-5-K, because it's the top kicker to an ace hand with nut-high and nut-low straight possibilities. Four low cards, like A-2-3-4, A-2-3-5, and A-2-4-5, with two suited cards, give you a chance of going low and wheeling (making a perfect low, a wheel—A-2-3-4-5) or flushing to a strong high hand.

When competing for the high end of the pot, hands with A-K and A-A have more strength against fewer opponents and less value against more opponents, since straights, flushes, and full houses are more common as more players stay to the end. You can start with some high-only hands, but if you do, all four of the cards must be coordinated, that is close in rank to one another. Thus, a hand like K-K-Q-J would be good, but K-K-Q-7 would not. That 7 is a **dangler**, meaning that it doesn't coordinate with the other cards.

THE FLOP AND BEYOND

When the three-card flop hits, it's important for you to reevaluate your situation. The more players remaining to see the flop, the better your hand must be. In particular, you either need to have the nuts or a draw to the nuts, because with the loose action common in many games, especially low-limit ones, that's what it's going to take to win.

When you're unsure of how to proceed with a hand, remember position. If you're early and vulnerable to raises behind you, you have an easy fold. If you're late, you can see what develops.

High starting hands of A-A-K-Q and A-A-K-K remain strong if the flop is all high cards, preventing low hands from taking half the pot, which would immediately devalue the pot by one half. This is a key concept that players going for the high end of the pot must consider in Omaha 8-or-better. Also, for any player to qualify for a low total, there would have to be three low cards (8 or below) on board.

Key tip for the high end of the pot:
If two low cards or fewer are on board,
there will be no low hand, and the high hand
will take the whole pot.

When making your decision on how to play a high hand, you must consider that the pot is only worth half of what you might normally expect if a low possibility is on board. The dilution of the pot is something that regular high or low players often overlook, but it affects betting and playing strategy. That is why hands with the strength to go both ways are so valuable in high-low games.

If you don't connect with the flop, especially with

high-only cards, drop your hand. If you do connect, make sure your hand is going toward the nuts and not second best. With more betting rounds to come, you don't want to be putting in a lot of chips unless you have a hand that can go all the way.

11. DRAW POKER

Draw poker is typically the first poker game players learn. The high version of the game is predominately played in casual home poker games among family and friends and rarely, if ever, dealt in a cardroom anymore. The low versions of draw poker games, however, still can be found in cardrooms, though with the recent popularity of hold'em and Omaha, these games are becoming more rare.

Online, however, where there is no overhead in hosting the games, you'll find draw poker games on some sites.

Though draw poker is typically played in a limit betting structure, no-limit structures are dealt as well; in fact, the 2005 WSOP lowball event was played as no-limit.

In this chapter, we'll cover four draw poker versions: jacks or better, anything opens, lowball, and triple draw.

OVERVIEW

In draw poker, each player is dealt five face-down cards to start, and there are two betting rounds. These cards are known only by the holder of that hand. The first betting round occurs after the initial cards are received and before the **draw**, when players have an opportunity to exchange unwanted cards for new ones. In cardroom draw poker, players may exchange up to five cards. In some home games, players are restricted to drawing three cards, unless they have an ace and can draw four cards to it, but this is unusual.

After the first round of action is completed, there is a draw, which is followed by a second round of betting, and then the showdown. At the showdown, the highest hand wins the pot. If all other players have folded, the last remaining player is the winner.

Draw poker is sometimes played with an ante and sometimes with a blind, a mandatory bet placed by two players (sometimes three, sometimes only one). Rarely, both a blind bet and an ante are used as part of the structure.

JACKS OR BETTER

Both the casino and private versions of jacks or better require antes. These must be placed into the pot before the cards are dealt. Antes usually range from 10% of the maximum bet (normal size) to 20% (considered a high ante). For example, in a $5/$10 game, a $1 or $2 ante would be typical.

To open the betting in **jacks or better**, which is also known as **jackpots**, a player must have a hand with a minimum ranking of a pair of jacks, called **openers**, in order to open the betting. For example, a pair of queens, three deuces, or a straight are hands that could open betting, while a pair of sevens or an ace-high hand could not. If you hold a jacks-or-better hand, you do not have to open betting, however. You may check your turn.

Any player, even one with openers, can elect not to open. Once an opening bet is made, subsequent players can call, fold, or raise the opener. Checking is no longer permitted. If all players check on the opening round of play, the hand is said to be **passed out**. If that occurs, the cards are collected and shuffled, and the next player in turn gets the dealer's position. New antes will be required of all players and these will be added to the ones already in the pot.

THE PLAY OF THE GAME
The player to the immediate left of the dealer will receive the first card with the deal continuing clockwise, one card at a time, until all players have received their allotment of five cards. The first round of betting begins with the player on the dealer's left.

THE FIRST ROUND OF BETTING
The first player to act must check if he cannot open betting or chooses not to open. The next player, in turn, must also check if he doesn't hold the requisite opening cards. Players continue checking until an opening bet is made. Subsequent players must call that bet to play for the pot, raise the bet, or fold. Checking is no

longer permitted. Play continues around the table in a clockwise fashion until all bets and raises have been called.

THE DRAW

The draw occurs after the first betting round is completed. Each remaining player, beginning with the first active player to the dealer's left, can exchange unwanted cards for new ones. The cards should be tossed face-down toward the dealer, who will issue an equivalent number of new cards from the unused portion of the deck. You should draw in turn, waiting for the previous player to receive his new cards before making your own discards. The dealer position draws last, if he is still in the pot.

Discards should be announced, so that all players are aware of the number of cards drawn. Players who do not draw any cards are said to be **standing pat**. You can indicate your choice to stand pat verbally or by knocking on the table with your hand.

THE SECOND ROUND OF BETTING

The second round of betting follows the draw. It is begun either by the opener or the last raiser, if there were any raises during the round. If no raises occurred, and the opener has folded, the first active player to the dealer's left opens the betting. This player may check or bet as desired. Each succeeding player has the option of checking or betting, but once a bet is placed, active players must call, raise, or go out.

DRAW POKER

THE SHOWDOWN

The showdown occurs after the second betting round is completed. At this time, the player who was the last to bet or raise turns over his cards first. Any opponent who claims a superior hand must show his cards while players holding inferior hands may go out without revealing what they hold. The best hand wins the pot and gets to rake in the chips.

SAMPLE HOME GAME

Let's return to our original crew and see how the betting works in a $5/$10 limit game of jacks or better played as a Friday night home game. They're playing with a $2 ante, a high ante for these betting limits, and one which encourages "stealing the antes." The pot holds $16 to start (eight players times $2).

These are the cards they hold after the deal:

Julian	K	10	7	3	2
Eddie-boy	8	8	10	4	2
Vicenzo	A	A	J	10	8
Fay	6	6	A	4	3
Donto	A	J	7	6	3
Flavian	K	10	9	8	7
Uncle J.	J	J	5	4	2
Big Phil	5	5	5	8	7

Julian sits to the immediate left of the dealer, so he opens play. Not having a hand of jacks or better, Julian checks, as does Eddie-boy, who holds only a pair of eights. Vicenzo can open, and he does, flipping a $5 chip into the pot. Fay has nothing worth betting on, and she folds.

Donto is excited enough by his ace-high hand to call the bet, but it's a poor play. He's a big underdog with those cards and has little chance of winning.

Flavian's cigar is blowing smoke like a train coming down the tracks. With two players in the action and a large ante, the $25 in the pot gives him good pot odds to go for his straight (26-5, greater than the approximately 4-1 odds he needs to make the play justifiable), and he calls the $5 bet as well.

Uncle J. knows that the opener, Vicenzo, holds jacks or better, and he figures that Vicenzo, who is a solid player, probably has at least kings or aces to have opened in such an early position. With two other players in the game, he folds his pair of jacks. He figures they're of little value and not worth a bet.

Big Phil tosses $10 into the pot, calling the $5 opener and bumping that bet $5 more. His three fives are strong cards. If too many players are allowed to draw out against them, the possibility of them getting beat increases.

Julian and Eddie-boy see that their free ride is over and fold in turn. Neither thinks his cards are worth a $5 bet, let alone a $5 raise on top of that. Vicenzo calls the raise and flips his $5 into the pot. Donto finally folds, $5 poorer thanks to his earlier call. Flavian is playing for the draw and calls the $5 raise. The raise has now been called by all active players, and the betting is over.

On this first round of betting, before the draw, all bets and raises are in the lower tier of the $5/$10 game. After the draw, all bets will be in the upper tier, or in $10 increments.

Three players remain for the draw: Vicenzo, Flavian, and Big Phil. Vicenzo throws his discards toward the dealer and draws three cards to his aces. Flavian calls for one card. When it is his turn, Big Phil takes one card as well. Though Big Phil theoretically has better chances of improving his hand with a two-card draw, his one-card draw is a clever play, since opponents probably figure him for two pair. Meanwhile, he's sitting pretty with his three fives, a favorite against two opponents.

Here's how the hands look after the draw:

Vicenzo	A	A	9	9	2
Flavian	10	9	8	7	4
Big Phil	5	5	5	K	6

The opener, Vicenzo, acts first and bets $10. His aces over nines is a strong hand, and he figures it's a stronger hand than Big Phil's probable two pair. Flavian's train has slowed down, and he folds. The 4 that he drew fell short of his needs. There's not much he can do with a 10-high hand.

Big Phil raises the bet to $20 (a $10 raise) and Vicenzo calls the bet. Since Vicenzo called Big Phil's raise, Big Phil must show his cards first. He turns over his trip fives. Vicenzo sees that he is beat, throws his cards face down and concedes the pot.

Big Phil is the winner. He collects all the chips in the pot, giving them a new home in his private stack. A new deal is ready to begin.

STRATEGY FOR JACKS OR BETTER

As with all other poker variations, the single most important strategy in jacks or better is to start out with cards which have good winning possibilities. The opening requirement of jacks or better tells you right off that any pair less than the minimum opening hand of jacks is automatically a big underdog. For example, if an opponent opens the betting, what chance would your pair of eights have, given that your opponent must have at least a pair of jacks?

Position is an extremely important consideration in jackpots. The dealer position has the biggest advantage because he not only acts last in the first betting round, but gets to exchange cards after all other players have made their drawing decisions. With marginal hands, you can come into the pot cheaply, or if the action is too stiff, you can fold. You're in a great position to bluff, and being the last to draw, you can make use of your drawing strategy to gain a powerful edge. Due to the dealer's big positional advantage, draw poker is an excellent choice in dealer's choice games.

The relative position you have at the table affects the types of hands that you should play and how they should be bet. For example, if you open betting with a pair of jacks or queens in an early position, you're in a bad situation if you get raised by several players. You have to figure the raisers for at least kings or aces, possibly better, and your lowly pair of jacks becomes a big underdog and must be folded.

Let's examine the minimum requirements for profitable play in jacks or better.

Jacks or Better · Minimum Opening Cards	
First Four Positions (Early):	Kings or Better
Second Two Positions (Middle):	Queens or Better
Last Two Positions (Late):	Jacks or Better

In late position, when no openers have yet been made, the pair of jacks becomes a stronger hand. The jacks take on greater value in late position in a hand without openers, and have the advantage in that your opening bet might force opponents out of the pot and win the antes. If only one or two players call the opener, the jacks are in a decent enough position going into the draw to have a realistic chance of winning the pot.

Once someone has opened the betting, players holding jacks or queens should call only if two players or fewer are in the pot and no raises have been made. Otherwise, jacks and queens should be folded. Their winning chances diminish as the number of active players increases.

Four-card straights and flushes have good potential. They should be played to the draw, but only if the pot odds justify calling the bet. (See Winning Concept #7 in the Twenty-One Winning Concepts of Poker chapter.) Do not raise with these hands, however. At this stage they're too speculative and hold little value. Should the draw fill these cards into a straight or flush, then you've got the goods to raise and build up the pot.

If you hold kings, aces, and low three-of-a-kind hands, you should not only call the opener but raise as well. These are strong cards. If you don't force out weaker and speculative hands, a lucky draw by inferior hands could bury your favorite, making you pay the price for playing weakly. Against fewer opponents, there's less chance of this occurring. The more players that stay in for the draw, the higher the average winning hand will be, and the greater the opportunity that the kings, aces, and small trips will get beat out by an inferior hand that draws good. You've got to raise when you hold strong cards—don't make the game cheap for dreamers.

On the other hand, with a high three of a kind, such as a set of tens or higher, don't raise—call! You have a strong hand which is favored to win without improvement. You want to keep as many players in as possible.

Do not play three-card straights or flushes, or inside straights. An **inside straight** is a four-card straight that has only one way of improving, such as 4-5-7-8. These longshot draws are chip burners and will lead to losing session after losing session if you continually try to chase with them.

PLAYING A SMALL TWO PAIR

Smaller two-pair hands, such as nines over threes, are deceptive hands in draw poker and must be played carefully. At first glance, two small pairs appears to be a strong hand with good winning possibilities. In reality, however, these cards can be trouble.

While a small two pair may stand tall before the draw against three opponents, that hand becomes an underdog after the draw. If you're facing bets and raises before the draw and more bets after it, your small two pair (with 11-1 odds against improving) starts looking even smaller.

Fold two small pairs in early position if the pot is opened ahead of you. Do the same if you're in late position and three or more players are in the pot. In the latter case, raising the pot by one extra bet probably won't force your opponents to fold, but it will open you up to a reraise. This is asking for a tricky situation to get more expensive than you'd like. In last position, however, against just one or two players, you should raise, and try to get rid of them. You have good position after the draw, which works to your advantage, and fewer players to outlast.

THE DRAW

There is a lot of strategy involved in drawing the correct number of cards, though for the most part, the correct strategy is straightforward.

When you're drawing to a pair, your best odds of improving is to take a three-card draw. Sometimes, however, holding a kicker can be a powerful bluffing tool. Opponents have to suspect your two-card draw for three of a kind. Occasionally, using the kicker in this fashion can disguise your hand.

Drawing one card to a three of a kind is a good bluffing strategy as well. Let's say you're playing a $5/$10 game. The first two players check and the third player opens with a $5 bet. The next player folds. You're in the next seat holding three eights, and you raise the opener $5. Players fold in turn around the table. Only the opener calls your bet. He goes first and draws one card. You take one card as well.

After the draw, the opener bets $10, probably holding kings or aces up and figuring you for a lower two pair. You raise $10, banking on the 11-1 odds against his improving. He calls. Then he quickly folds his cards after you turn over your three eights.

Fold four-flushes and four-straights if they don't improve at the draw.

DRAW POKER: ANYTHING OPENS

Draw poker: anything opens is played the same as jacks or better except that any hand may open the betting, regardless of strength. For example, a pair of sevens could open betting in anything opens, or even a queen-high hand. Otherwise, the rules and methods of play are identical to jacks or better.

STRATEGY FOR ANYTHING OPENS

The strategy in anything opens is virtually the same as in jacks or better. Though any cards can open the betting, don't be fooled into opening or calling bets with anything less than you would play in jackpots. No matter what the opening requirement, you'll be dealt just as many good and bad hands in one game as in the other. The same minimum starting hands apply here as in jacks or better.

Odds Against Improving Draw Poker Hands

Cards Held	Cards Drawn	Improved To	Approximate Odds Against
One Pair	3	Two Pair	5.3-1
		Three of a Kind	7.8-1
		Full House	97-1
		Four of a Kind	360-1
		Any Improvement	2.5-1
One Pair plus kicker	2	Two Pairs	4.8-1
		Three of a Kind	12-1
		Full House	120-1
		Four of a Kind	1,080-1
		Any Improvement	2.8-1
Three of a kind	2	Full House	15.3-1
		Four of a Kind	22.5-1
		Any Improvement	8.7-1
Four-Card Straight (Open Both Ways)	1	Straight	5-1
Inside Straight	1	Straight	10.8-1
Four-Card Flush	1	Flush	4.2-1
Four-Card Straight Flush (Open Ended)	1 1	Straight Flush Straight or Better	22.5-1 2-1
Four-Card Straight Flush (Inside)	1	Straight Flush Straight or Better	46-1 3-1

DRAW POKER: LOWBALL

This interesting draw poker variation presents a different twist to poker. The lowest hand is the strongest in **lowball**, or **loball** as it is sometimes spelled, as opposed to the standard high poker game in which the highest hand is the best.

In the ace-to-five version, the ace is still the best lowball card, but unlike in high poker, in which the ace counts as the highest card held, in ace-to-five the ace counts as the lowest card of a hand. The 2 is the next lowest card, and therefore the next best lowball card, and is followed in order by the 3, 4, 5, and so on, up to the king, which is the worst card. (See the next section, Triple Draw, for a discussion of deuce-to-seven low poker.)

In ace-to-five lowball, the highest card counts in determining the value of a hand; the lower the highest card, the better the hand. Hands are announced by their two highest cards. For example, the hand 7-6-4-2-A is announced as a "7-6" or "7-high," and 8-4-3-2-A is announced as an "8-4" or "8-high." Of the two above-mentioned hands, the "7-6" is the more powerful lowball hand, since its highest card, the 7, is lower than the 8, the high card of the "8-4" hand.

In instances where the highest ranks of two hands are of the same value, the next highest cards of the hands are matched up, and the lowest value of these matched cards determines the winner. Thus, the hand 8-6-4-3-2 is stronger than 8-7-3-2-A, and 9-6-5-2-A beats

9-6-5-4-A. When competing hands are equivalent, such as 8-5-4-3-A versus 8-5-4-3-A, the hand is a tie and the pot is split.

The **wheel** or **bicycle**, 5-4-3-2-A, is the perfect lowball hand. It can never be beat. At best, it can be tied by another wheel. 6-4-3-2-A is the next strongest lowball total, followed in order by 6-5-3-2-A, 6-5-4-2-A, 6-5-4-3-A, 7-4-3-2-A, 7-5-3-2-A, and so on.

Since straights and flushes do not count against the low hand, the wheel, 5-4-3-2-A, is not considered a straight. It's a perfect "5-4." An 8-4-3-2-A, all of hearts is simply an "8-4" hand, not a flush as it would be in high poker.

Any five-card hand containing a pair is a weak hand and can be beat by any five unmatched cards. For example, K-Q-7-6-5 is a winner over 2-2-3-4-5. Two pair, three of a kind, full houses, and four of a kind are increasingly worse holdings. The odds of these hands winning a pot in lowball are steeper than a canyon wall.

The term **smooth** in lowball refers to a hand with a relatively good back four cards, such as the hand 9-5-4-3-A, a smooth nine. **Rough** suggests a relatively weak back four cards, such as the hand 9-7-6-5-2, a rough nine.

DRAW POKER

THE PLAY OF THE GAME

Lowball is played similarly to high draw poker, with two betting rounds, one before the draw and one after. An ante is often used as well, and that bet should be placed into the pot before the cards are dealt. When no ante is required, a blind bet is used. Sometimes both a blind bet and an ante are used.

The order of play and betting proceeds as in the other draw poker variations. At the showdown, the lowest hand wins the pot. The deal now moves to the left. In the case of a casino game, the former blind is now the button and can enjoy all the advantages of playing the dealer's position.

STRATEGY FOR LOWBALL

The knowledgeable player has a tremendous advantage over beginners at this variation, since the strategic thinking is vastly different from high poker. In lowball, players are shooting for different types of hands, and it takes the high poker player some time to become accustomed to the peculiarities of playing for low hands.

The cardinal rule in lowball is this: never play a hand which needs more than one card drawn to improve to a winner. Unlike high poker, draws of two, or even three cards are terrible draws and immediately single out a player as a weak opponent. A two-card draw is a shot in the dark. It's equivalent to trying to fill a three-card straight in high poker.

To win at lowball, you must start out with cards that can win. If the cards you're dealt are weak, throw them away unless you can get a free ride. For example, if you're the blind, and there are no raises following the forced bet, it costs nothing more to play, so you should stay in for the draw. Always play further if there is no cost, no matter the cards. However, if you're faced with a bet, fold unless you've got the goods.

Position is important in lowball and must be part of your opening strategy. Here are the minimum opening cards you should play in lowball:

Lowball · Minimum Starting Cards

First Four Positions: (Early)	8-high—pat hand 7-high—one card draw
Second Two Positions: (Middle)	9-high—pat hand 8-high—one card draw
Last Two Positions: (Late)	10-high—pat hand 9-high—one card draw

---

Unless you hold an 8-high pat hand or have a four-card 7-high in early position, you can't call the blind's bet or make an opener yourself. You must fold. You're too vulnerable to raises behind your position to call with these hands in the first four spots. There is a strong possibility that players will up the stakes in the middle and late positions. It is foolish to call hands in middle and early position if you will be forced to fold on a raise. Do not call bets with anything less than the minimum openers in early and middle positions. In late position, if you're facing a bet and a raise, call with a minimum holding of an 8-high pat hand or a four card 7-high draw.

A 7-high pat hand is strong enough to play aggressively. Raise the opener from any position at the table. If a raiser enters ahead of you, reraise. When you're dealt a 6-high pat hand, you have an almost sure winner. Don't raise in early position. You want to keep as many players as possible in the game. However, if a player raises behind you, and it's just the two of you and maybe one other player, reraise and build up the pot. You're sitting pretty.

TRIPLE DRAW

Triple draw is a very fun variant of deuce-to-seven low poker in which the lowest and best card is a deuce and the highest, and therefore worst, is an ace. Flushes and straights count against the player, so the best hand is 7-5-4-3-2 of mixed suits, known as **number one**, with 7-6-4-3-2, 7-6-5-3-2, and 7-6-5-4-2 being the next three best hands. These are known, respectively, as **number two**, **number three**, and **number four**.

In deuce-to-seven, holding an ace is poison. Thus, 7-6-5-4-3 (a straight), and A-6-5-4-3 are terrible hands, beaten by the "lowly" hand of K-Q-J-9-8. And a 7-5-4-3-2 hand in clubs, a flush, loses to 4-4-4-K-Q!

There are three separate draws in triple draw, in which players get to replace unwanted cards with new ones. As opposed to the other draw poker variations, where there are just two betting rounds, one before the draw and one after, triple draw features four betting rounds—one when the cards are dealt, and one after each successive draw. Because of the number of cards needed, triple draw is played by a maximum of six players.

The four betting rounds of triple draw make the game very exciting, and that is why you will find it played by very high stakes players as part of a rotation of **mixed games**, in which multiple poker variations are played every turn around the table or by a preset time period. Triple draw is now a regular championship bracelet event at the annual World Series of Poker.

Triple draw, like hold'em and Omaha, uses a button to mark the dealer position, and is played with a small blind and big blind to stimulate action.

STRATEGY FOR TRIPLE DRAW

In triple draw, the first thing to keep in mind is that, with the four rounds of play, there is a tremendous amount of action. Triple draw is not for the faint of heart. Given the number of bets you'll have to face to see the showdown, you need to be very careful about the hands you choose to play and be prepared for big swings in your bankroll.

You also need to adjust your way of thinking if you're accustomed to playing ace-to-five lowball. For one, the ace is not the best card—it's the worst one. For another, you may end up with what you think is a great hand, only to realize that you're stuck with a straight or flush at the showdown! This results in a lot of lost chips. And unfortunately, these chips are going from you to your opponent and not the other way around.

So the first step toward acclimating yourself to this game is to realize that the deuce is boss. When you start out with a deuce, you have the potential for a great hand, and when you don't, you're working with a big handicap and should consider folding, especially against heavy betting.

STARTING REQUIREMENTS
Playing garbage in triple draw will soon divest you of a large portion of your chips, so your starting hand requirements must be very strict. I'll divide the starting hands into five categories: Pat Hands, One-Card Draws, Two-Card Draws, Three-Card Draws, and The Rest.

PAT HANDS
If you're dealt a five-card hand led by an 8, or even better, a 7, you should put in every bet you can in each round. Unlike other games, it is hard to disguise a big pat hand in triple draw because once it comes to the

draw and no cards are taken, it is no mystery that you're representing a big hand. A pat 8 can be vulnerable, but early on in the rounds, it is a probable favorite.

ONE-CARD DRAWS

One card draws to the 7 and 8 are strong and should be played aggressively. For example, K-7-5-3-2, K-6-4-3-2, Q-7-6-4-2, and A-8-5-4-3 are hands you can play aggressively. You should try to restrict the field by raising, thereby giving opponents fewer chances to get lucky and draw out on your cards. Your one-card draw is likely a better hand than any opponent holds, and you want those cards to stay in the lead. If you're drawing to the wheel (7-5-4-3-2), the best possible hand, you want opponents to stay in the pot, so you should play more conservatively.

An exception to playing one-card 8-draws is when a straight draw is possible, in which case your hand has problems. For example, A-8-7-6-5 and A-8-6-5-4 reduces the number of good cards you can catch to two, as opposed to A-8-6-5-2, which gives you three good cards to catch.

If your five-card hand is led by a 9, and backed by strong cards, such as a 9-7-4-3-2, you have three draws to improve to a great hand. However, if your 9 is backed by big cards, such as 9-8-7-6-3, you have a hand that may be better thrown away.

DRAW POKER

TWO-CARD DRAWS

Most of the time you'll be drawing two cards to your hand, but you'll want to make this two-card draw to a good hand. Any three cards 7 or less which contains a 2 are strong, particularly 2-3-4 and 2-3-7, which are your best starting three-card hands. Two-card draws 7 or less with a 3 are less valuable, and should be dropped against heavy opposition, though they can be played against a late position player trying to steal your blind. Without the deuce, these hands drop in value, so on the draw, you're looking to get a deuce to improve.

THREE-CARD DRAWS

For three-card draws, the 2 must be one of those cards, along with a 3, 4, 5, or 7 (but not a 6, which is problematic). Otherwise your hand is simply not playable. Drawing three cards is a longshot, so you should make this play only if no one has entered the pot and you are in a steal position, or if you are defending the blind from a late position player you suspect of stealing. If you don't get at least one low card on the draw to improve your hand, you'll probably need to fold to any betting.

THE REST

If you need a four- or five-card draw to improve, muck your cards and wait for the next hand.

OTHER STRATEGY CONSIDERATIONS

The button acts last in every betting and playing round in triple draw, so like hold'em, position is extremely important. Pay attention to the number of cards opponents take before you have to draw, and watch how they bet before you commit any chips to the pot. If you were able to get position every hand you played, you would have an enormous advantage over opponents, especially given the fact that you'd not only be able to see the number of cards they draw before you have to make this decision yourself—as you would in other draw poker variations—but you'd get this advantage three times!

Whenever an opponent draws more cards than you, bet and force him to play for more chips. You have a big advantage and want more chips in the pot. Your opponents have that many more cards that could come bad, either high-carding or pairing their hands. If you draw more cards than your opponents, then the situation is reversed. Unless you improve, you should check in order to minimize the betting.

If you draw the same number of cards and improve, play aggressively. If you don't improve and go first, check. If opponents go first and bet, consider folding.

On the last draw, you have to keep in mind that your final draw could easily give you a pair, high card, straight, or flush, destroying a hand that was a strong four-card draw. For example, a 7-5-3-2, could turn into a woeful A-7-5-3-2 or even worse, 7-7-5-3-2. But you could also draw one of two great cards, a 6 or a 4, with an 8 being very strong and a 9, playable. Compare that to the hand

5-4-3-2 which gives you only one great card, a 7, one very strong card, an 8, and one playable card, a 9. The 6 would be a disaster, giving you a straight. 6-5-4-3 is even worse. This hand has nowhere to go. A draw of a 7 or a 2 destroys the hand by forming a straight, leaving you only with an 8 to make a relatively high 8.

On the last draw, if your opponent is drawing a card, a 9-high hand is a big favorite. In fact, if you have a five-card jack or better, you are a slight favorite over any opponent who has to draw one card. If your opponent draws first, you can consider staying pat with a jack-high hand because you're in the lead. However, if you go first with that same jack-high hand, you won't know what your opponent will do, so you should draw if your jack or 10 is backed by a four-card 8 or 7, and hope that your low improves. If you have a 9, you'll have to see how the action goes then decide whether a draw is needed. If your opponent stayed pat the draw before and you have a chance to improve, you'll probably need to take a card.

Always keep in mind that any one-card draw—either yours or your opponent's—can go down in flames with a bad card on the end. Until a made low is formed, the possibility of a disastrous draw is a risk in all the low poker variations.

12. SEVEN-CARD STUD

Seven-card stud's three main variations—high, low, and high-low—pack five exciting betting rounds into play. In each variation, each player forms the best five-card combination out of the seven dealt to produce his final hand.

In **seven-card high stud**, the highest ranking hand at the showdown wins the pot. In **seven-card low stud** (also called **razz**), the lowest hand claims the gold. And in **seven-card stud high-low** (and its variant, **seven-card stud 8-or-better**), players vie for either the highest ranking or lowest ranking hand, with the best of each claiming half the pot—with some restrictions, which we'll go into.

Players will receive a total of seven cards if they play through to the end. After the first three cards are dealt (two **face-down**, or **closed,** and one **face-up**, or **open**), the first betting round commences. The following three cards—the fourth, fifth, and sixth—are dealt open, one at a time, to each active player, with a betting round accompanying each card. The last card, the seventh, comes "down and dirty," that is, face-down.

All players who have not folded now hold three hole cards and four open cards. A final round of betting follows the seventh card, and then the showdown occurs with the best hand (or hands, as may be the case in high-low) claiming the pot. In each variation of seven-card stud, a player can also win the pot before the showdown by forcing out all opponents through bets and raises that opponents won't match.

THE PLAY OF THE GAME

All antes, if required, should be placed into the pot before the cards are dealt. Once an ante bet is placed, it is like any other wager. It is the property of the pot and will belong to the eventual winner of the hand.

The dealer distributes the cards in a clockwise direction beginning with the player to his left and continuing around the table, in order, until all players have received their initial three cards. Either the lowest open card on the table, or the highest, depending on the variation, is forced to make an opening bet, called a **bring-in**, which will start the action.

Play proceeds in a clockwise direction beginning with the player to the bring-in's left and moving around the table until all bets and raises have been called. Or it will end right there if no player chooses to call the bring-in, giving that first bettor the pot. This first round of betting is called **third street**, so named for the three cards that each player holds.

The bring-in bet is usually less than the size of the smaller bet in a limit game. For example, in a $5/$10 game, the bring-in might be $2. In seven-card stud high and high-low games played in cardrooms, the player holding the lowest open card makes the bring-in. If two players have identically ranked cards, the player with the lower ranked suit plays first. For this purpose only, the suits are ranked, with spades being the highest, followed by hearts, diamonds, and clubs. For example, if the lowest ranked open cards are the 3♣ and the 3♥, the 3♣ will open the betting.

In low stud games, razz, played in cardrooms, it is the opposite: the player with the highest ranking open card starts the betting. If two or more players hold equivalent values, the high-card player closest to the dealer's left will make the bring-in.

In high and high-low seven-card stud games played in home poker, the player with the highest ranking open card usually starts the betting, with the lowest ranking hand in home poker usually being the bring-in—and remember, the ace counts as the lowest card in low poker. But, as in all home games, players may use the high hand rather than the low one to open betting.

There is no checking on third street. The first player to the bring-in's left goes next, and he must either **complete** the bet, that is, bring it up to the lower limit of the betting structure (so if it's a $5/$10 game with a $2 bring-in, then he must raise $3 to make it $5), raise the completed bring-in, or fold. All bets and raises in this first betting round are at the lower limit of the betting tier. So if you're playing a $5/$10 game, all bets would have to be for $5. If a player wants to raise the completed bring-in, it would be by $5 more, making it $10 to the next player.

When third street betting is completed, each active player receives a face-up card. Everyone now holds a total of four cards, two open and two closed. Play in this round, called **fourth street**, and all the following rounds, whether in a home game or a cardroom, begins with the best open hand and moves clockwise around the table. In high and high-low seven-card stud, the best hand is the highest ranked, and in low poker, the best hand is the lowest ranked. When two or more players hold identically ranked cards, the player closest to the dealer's left plays first.

For example, in low poker, a player showing 8-6-2-A on board, an 8-6 hand, would act before a player showing a pair of sixes, 6-6-3-2. Similarly, a 6-4-2-A board would open against a 7-3-2-A. And if players held K-K, A-Q, and 6-6 in a high or high-low game, the pair of kings would lead off the betting.

Beginning on fourth street, which is the second betting round, and continuing through the last betting round, the first bettor to act may check to open the betting since there is no bring-in bet to meet. It is only on third street that an opening bet is required for players to stay in active competition for the pot. All bets and raises on fourth street are in the lower limit of the betting structure unless an open pair shows on board, in which case players may elect to open with a bet from the upper limit of the betting. Thus, on fourth street in a $5/$10 game, bets would be $5, unless an open pair forms on board, in which case $10 could be bet.

Once fourth street betting is concluded, another open card is dealt to each active player. Players now have a total of three face up cards in addition to their two down cards. This round is called **fifth street**, and all bets and raises on this round and on the following two rounds, sixth and seventh streets, are in the upper tier of the betting limit. In a $5/$10 game, bets and raises would be $10, in a $3/$6 game, $6, and in a $15/$30 game, $30.

After this round of betting closes, active players receive their fourth open card. This next betting round is called **sixth street**, so named for the six cards each player holds. It is played like fifth street, with the highest ranking open hand acting first and concluding either when all bets and raises have been called, or when all opponents fold, ceding the pot to the last remaining player.

Seventh street is the final betting round. Each remaining player receives his seventh and final card face-down. There is a round of betting, which is followed by the showdown if two or more player remain.

THE SHOWDOWN: HIGH STUD AND RAZZ

In straight high poker and low poker, each player chooses five cards out of the seven total he holds to form his best hand. In seven-card high stud, the best high hand wins, and in the lower stud version, the five best low cards will claim the pot.

THE SHOWDOWN: HIGH-LOW STUD

The main difference between high-low stud and straight high or low versions, is that you're actually playing for two parts of the pot: half the pot goes to the player with the best high hand and the other half goes to the player with the best low hand.

High-low seven-card stud is played as either "cards speak" or "declare." In **cards speak**, which is the style universally played in cardrooms, players simply reveal their cards at the showdown—like all other poker variations. The best high hand and the best low hand split the pot, or if one player is fortunate enough to have the best high and low, he'll claim it all or scoop. In **declare**, which is only played in home games, players announce at the showdown whether they're going for the high, the low, or the high-low end of the pot, and they're committed to that declaration.

High-Low Declare

A player declares his intentions by hiding a colored chip in his fist and extending his closed fist over the table. At a given signal, players simultaneously open their hands and reveal their decisions. White chips are usually used for a low declaration, blue chips for high, and red chips for high-low, though using different color arrangements, coins, or writing the decision on a folded note will work just as well.

If a player declares high and loses to a higher ranking-hand, but actually has the best low hand, he gets nothing because he didn't declare low. Players are only eligible for the part of the pot they declare.

Among the players who declared "high," the best high hand wins that half of the pot, while the best low hand among players who declared "low" takes the other half. If just one player calls "high" and the rest "low," the player declaring high automatically wins half the pot and need not show his hand, while the low declarers compete for the other half—and vice versa. If all players declare high, then the best high hand wins the entire pot. If all players declare low, then the best low hand claims the entire pot.

Players that declare "high-low" risk all, and must have both the best high hand and the best low hand or they forfeit the entire pot. It's an all or nothing proposition. If a high-low declarer wins only one way, then he's out of the pot, and the best high hand and the best low hand split the chips. And if just one opponent remains against the high-low declarer and the one-way declarer wins his side of the pot, he gets the entire pot since the high-low hand failed to win both halves.

Sample Declaration

Let's follow a showdown in a game being played as declaration. Five players remain: Donto, Fay, Julian, Eddie-boy, and Big Phil. The first three declare "high," the fourth "low," and the fifth, Big Phil, goes all out and declares "high-low." (Flavian has already folded and both he and his cigar watch passively from the sidelines.)

Donto (Declared high)   J♣ 10♠ 9♦ 8♥ 7♣

Fay (Declared high)   K♥ K♣ K♦ 5♣ 4♥

Julian (Declared high)   A♦ 10♦ 8♦ 6♦ 3♦

Eddie-boy (Declared low)   7♦ 6♥ 4♣ 3♥ 2♥

Big Phil (Declared high-low)   High: K♠ 7♠ 5♠ 4♠ 2♠

                                  Low: 7♠ 5♠ 4♠ 3♣ 2♠

Big Phil's 7-5 hand is a stronger low than Eddie-boy's 7-6, but his king-high flush is weaker than Julian's ace-high flush. Therefore, Big Phil, unable to win both ways, loses his high-low declaration and wins nothing. Julian and Eddie-boy hold the best high and low hands respectively, and they split the pot. Had Big Phil declared "low" only, he would have won that half of the pot.

SEVEN-CARD STUD

SEVEN-CARD STUD 8-OR-BETTER

Seven-card high-low stud is sometimes played with a **qualifier**, a requirement that a player must have five unpaired cards of 8 or less to win the low end of the pot. If no player has an 8-or-better qualifier, then the best high hand will win the entire pot. For example, if the best low at the table is 9-6-5-4-2, then there is no qualified low hand and the best high hand will win the entire pot.

This version of seven-card stud low is called **seven-card stud 8-or-better**, or simply, **8-or-better**.

STRATEGY FOR SEVEN-CARD STUD: HIGH POKER

The first three cards you receive in seven-card stud lay the groundwork for the future possibilities of your hand. Therefore, to build winners, you should only stay in with cards that have the right winning ingredients. Starting and staying with promising cards is especially important in seven-card stud, since the five betting rounds of this game add up to a lot of bets and raises.

With all these chips at stake, you want to give yourself every chance of winning.

These are the minimum starting cards you need to enter the betting in seven-card high stud:

Seven-Card High Stud · Minimum Starting Cards

Three of a kind
Three-card straight flush
Three-card flush
Three-card straight
Pair of tens or higher
Low or middle pair with ace or king kicker
Concealed pair with face-card kicker
Three high cards, two of them suited

Starting cards of three of a kind are powerful hands that are heavily favored to win. With these cards, you want to keep as many players as possible in the pot. Play low key on third and fourth street, calling bets but not raising. If your opponents start showing threatening signs of flushes or straights on fifth street, bet heavy. You should either force them out or make them pay for the privilege of trying to buy their hands. However, if your trips turn into a full house, you have nothing to fear from straights or flushes. You want them filling their straights and flushes—and how!

With three-card flushes and straights, call third street betting, but do not raise. In general, it is prudent to raise only if you've either got the goods or you are bluffing (and only under the right circumstances). If your three-card straight or flush doesn't improve by fourth street, it's time to say goodbye. Fold the hand. The odds against filling it are getting too steep for the cost of calling bets and chasing cards for three more betting rounds.

One interesting thing about three-card flushes that most players don't realize is that when you end up winning with these cards, your winning hand usually is not the flush! Along the way, you'll make two pair hands, three of kind, a straight, full house, or perhaps a high pair. So it's important to remember that you prefer your three-flush to contain high cards. Holding a 10-7-4 flush draw is not as valuable as a K-J-2 flush draw.

For example, if the highest exposed card on board is a queen—say your opponent shows Q-J-10-7-5 on his board—pairing up your king in the hand K-J-2 gives you a much more competitive hand. If the showdown ends up matching pair against pair or two pair against two pair, your big pairs will often win.

As you can see, this is much more valuable than pairing up a 10, 7, or 4, weaker cards which form weaker pair and two-pair hands that often lose to bigger pair and two-pair hands. Of course, there are other considerations to take into account, but the high-card factor is one that must be considered from the get-go. Bigger is better.

Having a kicker to low and medium pairs is critical, and that is why you don't want to enter the pot without an ace or a king to support your weaker pairs. If you pair up the ace or king, it gives you a good chance to outlast opponents with smaller two-pair hands than you. Of course, if there is an ace on board, your king could be playing second-best so you need to be aware of that. But if you have an ace and pair it, you have at least the top pair, and are in pretty good shape. If your small and medium pairs haven't improved by fourth street, you'll probably want to toss the hand if an opponent raises the pot before your turn or bets with a higher pair on board. It's best not to chase hands when you're probably beat.

A key factor to winning at seven-card stud, or at any poker game for that matter, is making sure you lose as little as possible in the pots you don't win. You must fold hands which have not panned out or have become underdogs. Avoid the temptation to play "just one more card." That one more card costs money and if it's not a sound call, it's a bet deducted from your overall winnings.

To be a winner, you must wager with the odds, not against them. And those odds are defined by the cards held versus those of your opponents—not on the hopes of what might happen. Again, when a promising hand's possibilities wither and it looks to be second best, bury it.

Betting intensity can indicate the strength of your opponents' hands. If betting is heavy, with raises and re-raises, expect to see strong cards at the showdown. Heavy betting usually equates to strong hands. However, if the betting is relatively light, then the opposite applies: expect the average winning hand to be weaker.

You must pay attention to all the open cards in seven-card stud. Cards in play cannot be drawn and therefore greatly impact the chances that you or your opponent will improve your hand. For example, if an opponent holds an open pair of kings and you saw two kings folded earlier, you know that, no matter what kind of luck that player has, there's no way he can buy a third king.

On the other hand, your chances of completing a four-card flush draw are greatly diminished if you see that the six of the clubs you need have already been dealt to your opponents.

If you hold a marginal hand and are unsure of how to proceed, lean toward folding if cards you need are already in play, and lean toward playing if they are not.

STRATEGY FOR SEVEN-CARD STUD: LOW POKER (RAZZ)

In seven-card low stud or "razz" as the game is commonly called, you use your best five cards out of the seven dealt to form the lowest possible hand. Strategic thinking is *different* than in standard seven-card stud.

Unlike high poker, where players sometimes start with strong hands, good lowball hands always start out as **drawing hands**, hands which need improvement to develop into winners. (See the section on lowball in the draw poker chapter for hand rankings in low poker.)

Your first four cards may be A-2-3-4, a golden start, but if the next three cards you receive are two jacks and a king, then your hand melts into nothing. On the other hand, seven-card high stud presents situations where you're dealt big hands for starters, such as the starting hand Q-Q-Q, and regardless of the next four cards, these trip queens are heavily favored to win. Subsequent draws cannot diminish the inherent strength of this high hand. In contrast, lowball hands that don't improve die on the vine and become worthless.

To be competitive in seven-card lowball, you must enter the betting with strong starting cards, ones that can go all the way. Below are the minimum opening or calling hands that should be played in razz.

Seven-Card Low Stud · Minimum Starting Cards

Three-card 7-high or better (lower)
Three-card 8-high with two cards valued 5 or lower
Three-card 9-high with two of the other
      three cards being an ace, 2, or 3
An ace plus a 5 or a lower card, and an odd card

If you don't hold one of the above combinations, you must fold. You don't want to play underdog cards and contribute to other players' pots. If you can get a free ride into fourth street, take it, but hands weaker than those mentioned cannot call a blind or opening bet. However, if you're the blind, and no raises occur behind your position, you're already in—take the free card on fourth street.

Hands with relatively low supporting cards are called **smooth** hands. For example, the 3-2 in the starting hand of 7-3-2, a smooth seven, or the 4-3-2-A in the hand 8-4-3-2-A, a smooth eight. Hands where the supporting cards are relatively high are called **rough**, such as the 6-4 in the starting cards 7-6-4, called a rough seven, or the 7-5-4-3 in the hand 8-7-5-4-3, a rough eight. Smooth hands have greater possibilities of winning than their rough counterparts and should be played more aggressively.

If you make an 8-high hand or a smooth 9 on fifth street, you're in a strong position. You should bet and raise forcefully against players still holding drawing hands. You're the favorite, so you want to either force them out of the pot or make them pay for every card they try to catch.

Also, play aggressively against weak players when you've got the goods. They'll stay in too long with inferior hands. Why not make your winning pot that much larger?

STRATEGY FOR SEVEN-CARD STUD:
HIGH-LOW POKER

The splitting of the pot into two parts, half for the best high hand and half for the best low, makes seven-card stud an action-packed and exciting game. An astute player can win healthy sums against loose opponents, while a weak player can really get buried. Note that the advice in this section applies to both seven-card stud high-low (with no qualifier) and seven-card stud 8-or-better.

Though there are more ways to win at high-low stud, you must not let this tempt you into playing too many hands. The same winning principle applies here as in all poker games: enter the betting only with good starting cards, ones that have a good chance of winning. Staying in pots with hands that hold both high and low possibilities, but are mediocre in both directions, is a costly and weak strategy. You can work only with the cards that you're dealt.

Look for hands that give you possibilities of winning both the high and the low end of the pot, which is called scooping. The problem with playing one-way hands in high-low is that your bets immediately lose half their value due to the fact that you're going after only one half of the pot. If you get shut out, you lose all your chips. And if you win, you only get half of the action.

And what if you happen to get caught in a pot where one player has a lock on one part of the pot? You're going to get whipsawed for a lot of bets, making your pursuit of 50% of the action very costly if you're the player getting trapped, especially if you're the player drawing dead. The math is not favorable for you in many one-way pots.

So when you are playing for one-half of the pot, you need that hand to be very strong.

The best starting hand in seven-card high-low stud is three suited cards 8 or below (A, 2, 3, 4, 5, 6, 7, or 8), particularly if one of these cards is an ace or you have three consecutive cards for a three-straight flush. You have a great hand with excellent high and low potential and want to build the pot. If you're first in the pot, you should raise to build it up, but if you have raisers before you, just call.

Another big hand is a three of a kind, especially if the trips are low. This is a very deceptive hand. A pair of aces with an 8 or less to go with it, giving it two-way potential, is a strong hand as well. Other big pairs, like kings and queens, are almost worthless against an aggressive ace, as their scooping potential is limited and their high potential is vulnerable. In 8-or-better, big pairs take on more value because if low hands don't qualify, the high hand scoops the pot. However, you should never play a high hand that is not shaping up to be the best hand. This is an extremely important concept in high-low, with or without the qualifier.

Other strong two-way starting hands are three-straights 8 or less (A-2-3, 2-3-4, 3-4-5, 4-5-6, 5-6-7, and 6-7-8), three straights 8 or less with just one gap (such as 4-5-7 or 2-3-5), and three cards 8 or less that include an ace (such as A-4-5, A-3-8, and A-3-5). You can play these hands strong on third street, raising or handling a few bets before your position. You have a great shot at low, and if your ace pairs and there is no other ace on board, you have a good shot at the high as well.

Even if you don't pair, sometimes the ace by itself might be enough to win the high. For example, a player holding K-Q-K would have to consider folding against your ace if you bet aggressively since his one-way high hand is looking at a possible bigger pair.

If your three-straight 8 or less has two gaps and doesn't include an ace, such 4-6-8 and 2-4-6, it has some value but should be folded against heavy betting. If on fourth street, you're sitting with a four-card low topped by 8-7 or 8-6, you can't handle any action if another player looks like he's going for low as well—say by showing a 5-3 or 6-5 on board. And remember, an 8-led low hand is vulnerable against other players going low, particularly if you see no eights on their board.

You shouldn't play middle pairs without high kickers, three-flushes that don't have three cards 8 or less, three-straights with high cards (no scoop potential and only a draw to a high hand), and of course random cards that don't fit in with the starting hands discussed above.

SEVEN-CARD STUD

One important concept to keep in mind is that high hands can't turn into low hands, but low hands can turn into high ones if the right cards are drawn.

The nature of high-low stud calls for more aggressive play. When you have a chance to scoop the pot or you have a lock on either the high or low end of the pot, bet forcefully. You want to create big pots and make the winnings that much sweeter.

13. TOURNAMENT POKER

Tournament poker is a blast. It's great fun to outwit your opponents and win their chips, and it is even more fun when you survive long enough to win cash. And nowadays, with low-limit tournaments readily available in cardrooms around the country and major events like the big WPT and WSOP tournaments creating millionaires every month, there is a lot of excitement in the world of tournament poker.

While we are going to concentrate on no-limit hold'em tournaments in this chapter, the rules and structures covered here apply to all other tournament poker games you might play—limit hold'em, seven-card stud and Omaha variations, triple draw, and whatever other poker games might be offered.

HOW TOURNAMENTS ARE STRUCTURED

Tournaments are set up as a process of elimination. As players lose their chips and are eliminated from a tournament, the remaining competitors get consolidated into fewer tables. What might start out as a 200 player event played at twenty ten-handed tables will get reduced to nineteen tables, and then eighteen tables, and so on, as players bust out.

Eventually, the field will get narrowed down to just one table, the **final table**, where the prestige and big money is earned. And that table will play down until just one player is left holding all the chips—the **champion**.

REBUY AND FREEZE-OUT TOURNAMENTS

There are two types of tournaments—freeze-outs and rebuy tournaments. A **freeze-out tournament** is a do or die structure. Once you run out of chips, you are eliminated. Unlike a cash game, you can't go back into your pocket for more chips.

In a **rebuy tournament**, you can purchase additional chips, which is usually allowed only when your chip stack is equal to or less than the original starting amount and only during the first few specified rounds of play. This is called the **rebuy period**. Some tournaments allow limited rebuys, and others allow players to rebuy as often as they go broke, that is, until the rebuy period is over.

At the end of the rebuy period, most tournaments allow you to get an **add-on** as well—a final purchase of a specific amount of additional chips. Usually, only one add-on is permitted per player, though some events allow double add-ons, and rarely, even more.

Once the rebuy period is over, you're playing in pure survival mode. If you lose your chips, you are eliminated and your tournament is over.

COSTS OF ENTERING

Entry fees for tournaments can be anywhere from $10 to $25,000! Tournaments with entry fees under $100 are usually played as rebuy tournaments, while those with buy-ins greater than $1,000 are typically freeze-outs. The bigger money events like the ones you see on television featuring the top pros are almost always freeze-out tournaments.

TOURNAMENT STRUCTURE

Tournaments are divided into **levels** or **rounds**. Each level is marked by an increase in the amount of chips that players are forced to commit to the pot before the cards are dealt. The blinds slowly increase, and after a few levels, the antes kick in. Levels may be as short as fifteen or twenty minutes in low buy-in events that are designed to be completed in as little as a few hours, or as long as ninety minutes to two hours for major events that are structured to last up to a week. Players will typically be given a ten or fifteen minute break every ninety minutes or two hours in a tournament.

Each event is set up differently by the tournament director and the length of rounds and structure for increasing the blinds and antes will be posted in advance on a board or available on sheets you can pick up in the playing area, usually by the registration desk.

In general, the greater the amount of money at stake, the longer the tournament. Short, quick rounds such as those used in low-limit events, make for faster play and introduce a greater element of luck as players are forced to play more aggressively in order to stay ahead of the quickly increasing blinds and antes. In bigger events, players are given more chips to start, the rounds are longer, and increases in blinds and antes are more gradual so participants can get in a lot more play. This combination means that the skill factor plays a larger role in these tournaments.

Of course, in any tournament, no matter how big or how small—or any cash game as well—luck is always a factor. However, the greater your skill level and the better you play, the better your chances of getting into the money or winning the tournament. Yes, there is luck, but never downplay the amount of skill involved in succeeding in tournament poker. Once you play your first event, this will be eminently clear. And the more you play, the more you'll see how your decision-making creates your own destiny and your chances of winning the whole pie.

Sometimes the turn of a card can make or break your tournament, but the events that led up to the decisive moment, the number of chips you gained or lost, and the decisions you made have all played a part.

Below, is a fairly typical payout schedule. You'll notice that the first three rounds have only blind bets, and it isn't until the fourth round that ante bets kick in as well.

Levels/Antes/Blinds Chart #1

This sample structure gives each player $1,000 or $2,000 in starting chips.

Level	Ante	Blinds
1	-	25-50
2	-	50-100
3	-	100-200
4	25	100-200
5	25	200-400
6	50	300-600
7	75	400-800
8	100	600-1,200
9	200	800-1,600
10	300	1,000-2,000
11	500	1,500-3,000
12	1,000	2,000-4,000
13	1,000	4,000-8,000
14	2,000	5,000-10,000

Levels/Antes/Blinds Chart #2

This sample structure has $10,000 in starting chips.

Level	Ante	Blinds
1	-	50-100
2	-	100-200
3	25	100-200
4	25	150-300
5	50	200-400
6	75	300-600
7	100	400-800
8	100	600-1,200
9	200	800-1,600
10	300	1,000-2,000
11	400	1,500-3,000
12	500	2,000-4,000
13	500	3,000-6,000
14	1,000	4,000-8,000
15	1,000	6,000-12,000
16	2,000	8,000-16,000
17	3,000	10,000-20,000
18	4,000	15,000-30,000
19	5,000	20,000-40,000
20	5,000	30,000-60,000
21	10,000	40,000-80,000
22	10,000	60,000-120,000

STARTING CHIP COUNTS

Your starting chip total in a tournament is determined in advance by the tournament director. In low-limit events, a $30 buy-in might give you $500 in chips, though the tournament director could just as easily give you $200 or $1,000.

And in high-limit events, you'll typically receive the same number of chips as the amount of the buy-in. For example, in the main no-limit event of the World Series, players get $10,000 in chips for the $10,000 buy-in. And in WSOP preliminary events that cost, say, $1,000, players get $1,000 in chips.

But there are exceptions. In the $25,000 buy-in championship event of the 2005 WPT at the Bellagio, players received $50,000 in chips, and at another tournament, players were given $12,000 in tournament chips for the $10,000 buy-in. At yet another, a $10,000 buy-in netted players $20,000 in starting chips. So, as you see, there are many variations.

However, whether you are given $200 in chips, $1,000 in chips, or $10,000 in chips, you are on a level playing field with your competitors because in a tournament, everyone starts with the same amount of chips.

TOURNAMENT CHIPS

Unlike a cash game, where chips are the exact equivalent of money, tournament chips have no cash value. They may just as well be Monopoly money, because no one is going to give you anything for them outside the tournament. Thus, if you have accumulated $150,000 in chips and try to cash them out, all you'll get from the casino is strange looks and an explanation that all you have are tournament chips.

TOURNAMENT PRIZE POOL

Most tournaments are set up so that approximately 10% to 15% of all players (and sometimes as high as 20%) will win cash prizes. The number of places paid, those who finish **in the money**, is decided in advance by the organizers.

For example, if the size of the starting field is 300 players, the organizers might limit the cash payouts to the top 10%. Often, the payout will be rounded down to the number of full tables remaining so if the 300 person tournament was being played nine-handed, the event may pay the top three tables, or twenty-seven players.

The worst feeling in a tournament is being caught on the **bubble**—that is, being the last player eliminated before the money payouts begin. So if you're player number twenty-eight in the example above, you're very unhappy going home empty when every other player remaining wins money.

The payout structure is usually posted soon after the tournament begins, as the organizers add up the total number of entrants and figure out the number of places and amount paid to each money-winner.

If the structure will affect your decision to play, or if your curiosity can't wait the few minutes to the start time, you can approach the tournament director, and he'll have a good idea of how many places will be paid. Most players simply wait, however, until the announcement is made by the tournament director or on the television monitors that are typically placed in a location easily visible to the players. The monitors will usually list the number of places paid and the amount of money each finisher will win.

You can determine if the event is right for you by the entry fee and the potential prize pool. The greater the number of players, the bigger the prize pool. When the events are large, such as the $10,000 buy-in events, the prize pool often gets into the millions. These tournaments draw the top players you see on television, along with the amateurs trying their hand at winning the big money.

REBUY AND ADD-ON STRATEGY

During the rebuy period in an unlimited rebuy tournaments you could theoretically bust out after every hand and then rebuy for more chips. That can get expensive and make the cost of playing a low-buy-in tournament not so low-cost anymore. And the same goes for medium and high buy-in tournaments, where the original buy-in may turn out to be a mere fraction of the overall cost you end up paying.

A reasonable approach to rebuy tournaments is to

limit yourself to two or three rebuys. If you bust out after this, you can figure that it's just not your day and move on.

In a tournament, chips are power. A player with a lot of chips has a tremendous advantage over another player with less. When the rebuy period ends and you are given the option to increase your chip total with an add-on, you'll generally want to take advantage of this opportunity. If you have tripled your original chip count, you can consider riding with what you have, but even there, adding on for more gives you more power and a better chance to win.

Let's say you start a tournament with $1,000 in chips, build it up to $1,750, and decline an add-on at the end of the rebuy period. You will be at a tremendous disadvantage to a player who has that same $1,750 and picks up a $1,000 add-on to bring his stack to $2,750. And if it's a double add-on, a stack of $3,750 has a giant edge over you.

You cannot enter a rebuy tournament without being prepared to take on the additional costs of the add-ons. You simply must have enough money to purchase the add-ons available. You may decline to do rebuys and call your tournament finished if you bust-out—or at least limit your rebuys to one or two times—but if you're still in there when it's time to add-on, you have to be able to compete. And that means having enough for an add-on.

For example, let's say you pay $30 to enter an unlimited rebuy tournament which allows a double add-on at the end of the rebuy period, and the cost of each rebuy and add-on is $30. To keep yourself on an even playing field, you have to walk into the event with a bankroll of no less than $90. The first $30 is for the entry fee, and the next $60 is for the double add-on. If you plan on purchasing two to three rebuys, then you need to budget an extra $60 to $90. So your entry fee is not really $30—that's only your initial deposit—but $90 to $180, depending upon the number of rebuys you purchase.

You have more leverage over opponents when your risk of losing a big pot and being crippled is less than them. You also can't bust out against an opponent when you have more chips than he has. It's the law of the land in tournaments: big stacks have a big edge over little stacks. You must not lose sight of that concept when playing a tournament.

14. ONLINE POKER

Playing poker on the internet has become hugely popular. There are now millions of players from around the world competing against one another on hundreds of sites. With a few clicks of your mouse, you can get in on the action too.

It's easy to get started playing online. You begin by choosing a site and going to its homepage. From there, the instructions will guide you through all the basics: how to set up a unique account and password, how to play for free, and how to deposit funds into your account so that you can play for real money. There are some good things about online poker. Let's take a look and see what they are.

SEVEN ADVANTAGES OF ONLINE POKER

1. IT'S CONVENIENT

At any time of the day or night, all you have to do is go over to your computer, log on to your poker site of choice, and off you go. You're playing! There is nothing easier than that. It doesn't matter what you are wearing—or not wearing!—or how you look. You don't have to travel to a cardroom and search for the right game; with thousands of players online at any time, there is always a game with the stakes you want to play waiting for you.

2. IT'S GOOD SOCIAL FUN

Poker fires up that competitive spirit and is a great social outlet as well. You may not be able to see your opponents live, but that won't stop you from being able to communicate with them. Just as in a live game, you can interact with your tablemates. The chat windows in online sites allow you to type messages back and forth to your fellow players.

3. MAKE FRIENDS AROUND THE WORLD

Internet poker is now a worldwide phenomenon and it is not uncommon to see players at your table from a variety of countries. Like everything else, you eventually strike up friendships and you never know, you may soon be visiting some of your internet poker buddies—or receiving them. Many great friendships have started online.

4. IT'S GREAT PRACTICE

Online poker moves much faster than regular live games so you get to see lots of hands and situations. You can practice skills that you'll be able to apply to your regular tournament or cash game.

5. PLAY FOR MONEY OR PLAY FOR FREE

You can play poker for free on pretty much every site, a service online poker rooms offer their customers so they can get acclimated to the software. Or, if you prefer, you can sign up and play for real money.

6. IT'S PROFITABLE

Online players are generally much weaker than competitors you'll find in regular cash games, especially at the low limit games. This makes it very profitable for good players. If you're a really skilled player, it's more than a good way to make money, it's a great way to make a living!

7. IT'S GENERALLY SAFE

The main Internet poker sites are already established businesses with hundreds of thousands of satisfied customers. It is generally accepted that major sites provide games as honest as any poker room, if not more so.

QUICK ONLINE STRATEGY TIPS

Online players tend to play too many hands and see too many showdowns. You can profit from this by playing solid straightforward poker, extracting maximum value from your good hands and minimizing losses with your weak and marginal hands. With more players seeing the flop on average, you want to tighten up a little on the selection of hands you play.

Aggressive betting becomes even more important online, especially in no-limit. You need to limit the field to protect your premium hands. Avoid bluffing—you can't bluff players who won't fold—and give loose opponents less credit for having strong hands.

Like poker played in any form and in any setting, learning how your opponents play and adjusting your strategy accordingly will bring you the most profits.

One unique feature of online poker sites is the option players have to make a playing decision in advance, before play reaches their position by using the **early-action buttons**. And while there are no physical tells in online poker, the frequent use of these early-action buttons can give you information about an opponents' hands. For example, if you see almost instant checks or raises when the action reaches a player, quite often, that indicates that the player has pre-selected his action. In the first case, the check probably means he is weak, and in the latter, he is either strong or he decided that he was going to bluff at the pot regardless of the action that preceded him.

They key element here is that the player decided in advance what his play was going to be, without even considering how the betting might go. So with garbage, a player may select the Check/Fold button, which will fold his hand if there is a bet or check if there is not.

Also look out for players who frequently use the pre-select options and then break the pattern by taking time in a situation. That could be useful information, but at the same time, it could also be indicative that the player was busy doing something else—on the phone, checking email, or in another game! But do pay attention to the timing of an opponent's reactions, and you can pick up online tells that you can use to your advantage. And pay attention to your own tendencies as well. You're not the only one watching!

Once you get comfortable online, you may find it profitable to play two games at the same time, which will allow for lots of hands and lots of possibilities. Some action junkies (and pros) looking to maximize the number of hands they receive, may play up to three or four games simultaneously! If you are considering playing multiple games, which can get confusing, remember one key tip: avoid playing tricky marginal hands that show little long-term profit! The concentration you need to finesse victories with these marginal hands will be difficult when you're flying back and forth between multiple games. Profits in the other games will suffer as your concentration is focused on the marginal hand.

If you're a tournament player, there are an endless number of choices, some of which are for straight prize money and some which award seats to the main events in the World Series of Poker and World Poker Tour tournaments as prizes for the top finishers.

FIND OUT MORE

To find out more about playing on online poker sites, go to www.cardozapub.com.

15. TWENTY-ONE ESSENTIAL WINNING CONCEPTS

I've divided this chapter into twenty-one winning concepts that will improve your play and increase your profits at the table.

WINNING CONCEPT #1:
PLAY AGAINST COMPETITION YOU CAN BEAT

As with every competitive pursuit, being "good" at poker is a relative term. You may be a winning player at $5/$10, but if you move your chips to a $50/$100 game, you might get eaten alive. Similarly, while you may be a good basketball player at your local park, or a good chess player in your local club, if you change opponents and started playing against the pros, you might be a scrub unworthy to even be in the same game. And even those pros you might encounter wouldn't be good enough to be on the court with a Michael Jordan or across the board from a Garry Kasparov. The point is, there are levels of talent and ability. And when you go above your talent level, you create a mismatch.

Let me put this another way. If you're an average player and sitting at the big game with Doyle Brunson, Chip Reese, Lyle Berman, and company—and by the way, you'll need about $300,000 to have enough funds to do so—my betting money is not going to be on you. But if you are opposing a group of Martians who are playing poker for the first time, I just might back you. It's all about the level of competition.

In poker, you can't consistently win unless you're playing against competition at or below your level. If you play over your head, well, you'll be in over your head. It's one thing to be king guppy in a pond of guppies, but if you're moved into a bigger body of water, you'll soon realize that you're just a guppy to the bigger fish swimming there, one more scrap of food for them to swallow.

So, rule number one: play with players you can beat. Don't be a patsy for players who are just too good for you. Don't risk chips at a higher stakes game unless you're able to beat the opponents at your tables. Bear in mind this old poker saying: If you can't find the sucker in the game, you're it.

If you're unable to beat the level of game at which you currently play, don't move up a level thinking your "luck" will change. The only thing that will happen is that even better players will take your money at a faster clip. You'll be in way over your head. Move down instead. Get to a level where you can swim. You want to be the shark chasing the fish, not the fish being eaten.

For example, if you're at a $15/$30 game, and you're consistently taking a beating, get to the $5/$10 game, where your skills may be more equal to the competition. Improve your game there and when your skills improve—as measured by your winnings—go back and see what you can do at the higher stakes.

Take each level of poker in stride. You can make more money at a higher stakes game, but only if you're good enough to beat that game. A busy cardroom may offer games for $1/$2, $1-$5, $3/$6, $5/$10, $10/$20, $15/$30, $30/$60, $40/$80, $100/$200, 150/$300, or even higher. Just because higher stakes games are there doesn't mean you have to play them. Go slow, and work your way up as your skills improve. Earn it.

WINNING CONCEPT #2:
FOLD WHEN YOU'RE BEAT!

Winning money in poker is not just about winning pots. In fact, being an overall winning player probably has more to do with losing less when your cards don't come in the running than it has to do with the pots you win when you have the best hand! Many players don't appreciate this concept. They're winning enough pots, getting enough good hands, yet they can't understand why they keep leaving the table with losses.

Folding when you're beaten at the table is one of the most important concepts in poker. More money is lost by players who consistently make bet after bet in clearly losing situations than in possibly any other facet of poker. Every extra bet you contribute to an opponent's pot is one more bet out of your stack.

> ## Essential Concept
> *It's as important to make good folds in poker as it is to make good bets.*

To be a winner at poker, you must hold your money dear and value it like gold. There are good bets in poker, and there are bad bets. If you can cut the number of your bad bets in half, you'll be turning losing sessions into winning sessions and small winning sessions into larger winning sessions.

Do not play with cards that cannot win. Never lose sight of this concept when you're playing. When you lose, you should lose on hands you thought would be winners or which gave you good odds to play out as an underdog. Never lose with hands on which your odds of winning aren't worth the bets you're making; you shouldn't even be playing these cards.

Folding losing hands will make you more money at poker in the long run than any other strategic aspect of the game. In fact, it is essential if you're going to be a winning player. Getting rid of weak hands should not be interpreted as advice to play like a rock, to exit pots just because your hand is a dog, or to bet only when you're in the lead. Far from it. Smart poker play means balancing bets with your chances of winning, and that includes playing for pots when you're strong, when you're trailing, and sometimes—with the right pot odds or the right opponent—when you're weak.

When you do play second-best or worse hands, it should be because they give you good value, because your long term expectation is to win money in that particular situation. You may be an underdog in a hand, but if, in the long term, playing it gives you more profits than losses, you should play it. If the situation is ripe for a bluff and that might take down the pot, there is good value in betting or raising with a weaker hand. Your opponent may not fold, but if you estimate that he will fold enough times to make aggressive betting profitable in that type of situation, you have a good play. Playing only good hands will make you predictable and playing too many bad hands will bury you in losses. Profitable play requires you to strike a balance between the two extremes.

How do you know when staying in a hand is a correct play? It's not always easy to figure out just what the right move is in a game, even in hindsight, but that's what makes poker so fascinating. Experience and study will get you in the right direction.

Your goal in poker should be to win money. Competing in too many pots means you're making too many bets with too many inferior hands, for too long. Not good. This type of play will rapidly drain your bankroll; this is *not* a winning long term strategy. Usually, it's not a good short term one either. Learning to recognize when you're on the short end of the odds or are a big underdog in a hand will save you more chips than you can imagine.

WINNING CONCEPT #3:
PLAY WITH STARTING CARDS
THAT CAN WIN

Sometimes you're dealt playable starting cards; more often you're not. Obviously, in the first case, you'll play the good hands and see where they take you. But in the second instance, where your cards are not promising and you're a big underdog, the proper strategy is to fold.

Too many players start out with weak cards that have little hope of improving. They call other player's bets or initiate betting, putting themselves in situations where they can be raised and have to cough up yet another bet—all this when their hand doesn't warrant a single bet in the first place!

The object in poker is to have the best hand at the showdown, which means that to win you must enter into the betting with hands that have a reasonable chance of winning. While this appears perfectly obvious when you think about it, this concept is foreign to some players—and you like playing against these types of opponents because they're going to contribute to your pots. You won't win every hand you enter. If you did, there would rarely be any opponents contesting those pots. You must however, win enough money in the pots you do win to cover the losses from the pots you fall short in. To make this a mathematically sound principle, bet when you have a reasonable chance of winning, and fold when you don't.

The biggest mistake weak players make is playing too many hands. They're hypnotized by the action and don't want to miss any opportunities of catching a card that might make their hand a winner. Weak players call bets and raises with inferior hands, endlessly waiting for a golden card that will take them down the yellow brick road. Now and again, underdog hands will draw out to win pots, but the wizard won't always be there, and that type of play ultimately results in heavy losses.

You have to avoid the temptation to play poor starting hands just for the sake of getting action. If you're playing to win, you must be selective in the cards you play.

WINNING CONCEPT #4:
THE GOAL IS TO WIN MONEY, NOT POTS

There is a misconception among many players that winning more pots equates to being a bigger winner at the tables. In fact, the opposite is true! Weaker players tend to win more pots than stronger players because they're playing too many hands. Naturally, the more hands you play to the end, the more hands you will win, but that doesn't make for more profits. Every pot contested comes at a cost. When you contest many and lose many, it leads to a mighty bad day.

The goal is to win money, not pots. There is a significant difference between the two. After all, at the end of a poker session, you're not going to measure your results by how many pots you won. Winning money is what counts in poker—the final result. And winning money, not pots, should be your goal.

WINNING CONCEPT #5:
PLAY AGGRESSIVE POKER

Betting when there are no bets due and raising when there are puts pressure on opponents and forces them to commit more chips to stay in competition for the pot. One big advantage of aggressive play is that it often causes opponents to fold, giving you a "free" pot without having to face a showdown. When this occurs, you have a 100% chance of winning, and you can't beat that percentage. Aggressive play also allows you to narrow the field or isolate opponents.

Being heads-up gives you a much better shot of winning a pot than playing against three or more players. Now, you have only one person to beat. If two opponents enter pots with hands of equal strength, and play about the same way, you can expect similar results. With all else equal, you have a fifty-fifty shot of winning. Of course, all else will not always be equal. But in the long run, if you're heads-up and push at an opponent with another bet, your chances of winning increase beyond the fifty-fifty because of the increased likelihood that an opponent will fold and give up the pot. Aggressive play shifts the odds of winning pots. In a pot, the bettor or raiser is usually the favorite.

As you can see, aggressive betting (especially with good position) makes the math start looking better. When you play aggressively, your opponents tend to be more cautious, giving you more free cards when you want them, causing you opponents to fold more often when you bet, and making them more reluctant to lead out against you because they know you might raise them right back. Best of all, it makes your opponents more predictable, giving you a clearer picture of how to proceed when they play back at you.

Whenever you put pressure on opponents, it gives you the strength and your opponents the fear. Aggressive play lets you set the tempo of the game and forces opponents to play at your pace.

WINNING CONCEPT #6:
UNDERSTAND THE IMPORTANCE OF PLAYING POSITION

Your position at the poker table is an important consideration in whether and how you play your starting cards and in how you proceed in future betting rounds. Acting last is the best position at the poker table, and it gives you the biggest advantage on a hand. When you're last, you'll know the action you are facing and what it will cost to enter the pot before you have to commit any chips. This gives you leverage and flexibility to play a more aggressive game than early and middle position players. When there is a bet or raise early, signifying strength, you can fold marginal hands without cost. And when the action is light, marginal hands can be played more aggressively since few, if any, players will act behind your position.

There is less risk entering the pot from late position with bets or raises. With the appropriate hands or situations, you are in an excellent position to raise or bluff opponents out of the pot as a last position player. More antes and blinds are stolen from the last position and the seat acting before that spot than from any other position at the table.

On the other hand, holding marginal hands—which constitute the majority of hands you will be dealt—in early position, and less so in middle position, gives you no such choice. Perhaps you feel your hand is worth a bet, but certainly not two bets or more. The problem is that you cannot see what will happen after you bet and are vulnerable to raises and reraises. So you end up donating your chips by entering the pot early when raises behind your position force you to fold. Marginal hands are worth entering the pot only at a marginal cost. In early position, it is hard to gauge what your cost will be with a table full of players behind you.

When you are acting **under the gun**, that is, first, you are in the weakest position of all. You have no information about how opponents will play their hands after you, forcing you to fold hands you might otherwise like to play had you been in later position. The result is that early position players must play a more conservative and cautious game.

Essential Concept
The later your position, the more playable a marginal hand becomes.

Always consider how many players will act after your calls, bets, or raises, and how they might respond to your plays. The later your position, the more playable a marginal hand becomes. As a general rule, in borderline situations, be more likely to enter the pot in good position and to fold in bad position.

WINNING CONCEPT #7:
MAKE BETS WITH POT ODDS IN MIND

Pot odds is a concept that measures the risks against the rewards of making a bet—the risks being the cost of a bet, and the rewards being the amount of money to be won from the pot. For example, if the pot holds $100 and the bet to be called is $20, then the pot odds are $100 to $20, or 5 to 1. You use pot odds to determine if the cost of going for the pot is justified by the amount you might win. Let's look at an example to see how this works.

Let's say you're playing $10/$20 seven-card stud and two opponents are left. You hold aces over threes, and $40 is due your position. The first opponent, whom you figure for a three of a kind, has opened on sixth street with a $20 bet. The second player raised it $20 more. The second player sits with four hearts and has straight possibilities as well, good scare cards against your two pair. With the $40 worth of bets, the pot now holds $240. According to the pot odds, should you call?

Of course, you don't know for sure what cards your opponents hold, but your hand appears to be a loser unless it improves. You must draw an ace or a 3 to fill the two pair into a full house, which is the only way you figure to win the hand. However, the player with the heart-flush draw has one of your threes, and you noticed another 3 pass out of play earlier, leaving you, in fact, only two live cards, the aces.

A total of twenty-eight cards have been revealed: the eight open cards of your two active opponents, your six cards, and the fourteen cards folded earlier by the other players. That leaves twenty-four unknown cards. Only two of them, the aces, can help your hand. The odds of improving to be a winner are 2 in 24 (1 in 12), or 11 to 1 against. The pot offers only 6 to 1, poor odds against an 11 to 1 chance of improvement. Aces up might be a powerful hand in a different situation, but here, folding is the correct play.

The above hand worked well as an illustration, because just one card was yet to be played. This made estimating your pot odds relatively easy. Trying to do this calculation with more than one card to play becomes increasingly difficult as more unknowns come into play. How fast will the pot grow? What future bets will have to be called? What new cards dealt will change your projected strength versus your opponents? Though more variables may come into play and estimating pot odds may become less exact, a rough cost-of-playing versus money-to-be-won calculation is always helpful in determining whether a hand is worth committing more chips to.

The key thing here is that you don't have to make it too complicated. All you need is a general sense of risk versus reward, and as you get more experienced and comfortable with the concept, you'll get better at calculating the odds. For example, in draw poker, four-card straights and four-card flushes are unprofitable and should be folded before the draw if two opponents or fewer are in the pot. The chances of improving these four-card totals to a straight or flush are approximately 4 to 1 against. With less than three players in contention, the money in the pot is generally not enough to justify the cost of the call.

Sometimes, the size of an ante can affect the pot odds enough to alter a decision. For example, let's say you're playing a $5/$10 draw poker game with eight participants and a $1 ante. The pot initially holds $8 worth of antes. If only one player calls the opener, these two $5 bets boost the pot up to $18 in bets and antes. With only $18 to win and a cost of $5 to call, the pot offers less than the 4 to 1 odds needed to make calling a good play. The smart move here is to fold. On the other hand, if the above game were played with a high ante, say $2 per player, calling would be the proper play. The $10 in bets added to $16 in antes ($2 ante per player times eight players), fills the pot with $26 in bets and antes. Those are odds of 26 to 5 on the bet, better than the 4 to 1 odds needed to justify the call. Playing to the draw in this situation is an excellent move.

While evaluating pot odds is not always an exact science, it is a useful and important evaluation tool that will help you make profitable strategic decisions in poker.

WINNING CONCEPT #8:
LEARN TO SPOT TELLS AND WATCH OUT FOR YOUR OWN

There is a psychological and emotional reaction to every stimulus and event that occurs at a poker table—and a resultant physical expression of that reaction. The reaction can be expressed in some form of body language, like a player shifting in his seat, leaning forward, or scratching his head. It could be a small facial expression like a twitch, a tightening of the eyes, a vein pulsing, or perhaps a faint grimace. It could be breathing patterns or a certain stillness. Unless you're playing a carcass—and my question would be, "Why are you playing a carcass?"—the body reacts to stimuli, in one way or another.

In poker, an inadvertent mannerism or reaction that reveals information about the strength of a player's hand is known as a **tell**. There is a science and an art to figuring out opponent's tells and this information, when gathered, is very valuable. Every player has tells, some more disguised than others. It is not only your objective to seek out the tells from your opponents, but to keep them from finding yours.

If you pay careful attention to the way opponents react to situations or how they behave when they lead out with a bet or make a raise at a poker table, you will occasionally pick up signs that will clue you in to the strength of an opponent's hand. For example, there are players that lose interest when they know they're going to fold. If they act after your position and you take a moment to observe them and pick up on this, you have gained valuable information. Other players feign a loss of interest and appear distracted when they actually hold monster hands.

You'll often see beginners grabbing their chips when they know they're going to call a bet, even though the action is several players in front of them. Some players watch the action more closely than normal when they know that they will be participating in the betting. Players may hold their cards differently or wear a different expression when they're going to fold. Other players can scarcely contain their excitement when they're dealt a big hand, and they may express this in all sorts of obvious mannerisms—obvious, that is, if you're watching their reactions. Some players act weak when strong, and strong when weak. There are thousands of tells available for you to take advantage of, but you have to be observant and pay attention to your opponents to pick up on them.

Look for vocal patterns and tones, how players handle their chips or pass time toying with them, the way they hold their cards, their facial expressions. You should also watch where an opponent's eyes go. To his chip stack or an opponent's? To the pot, subconsciously counting the money he hopes to win? To other players' eyes, or at least to those of the one he fears most?

Watch everything: how a player sits, whether he speaks more or less—or louder or softer—than normal, whether he tosses his chips with more aggression than normal (bluffing?) or more meekly, or so that they barely make it into the pot (disguising strength?), whether he looks at you when betting or away. Does a player exhibit more movement when making an aggressive play, or less? Patterns will emerge.

Finding and using tells you discover in your opponents are worth a lot of chips to you. Having information on a player's intentions or an actual tipping off of an opponent's strength or weakness after he makes a bet is, needless to say, a huge advantage in poker. The classic book in the field, *Caro's Book of Poker Tells*, by Mike Caro, is the definitive book on the subject. It is highly recommended.

Learn to be consistent in your actions and develop a "poker face," so that when you've got the groceries, you can fill the bag.

WINNING CONCEPT #9:
DISGUISE YOUR BETTING ACTIONS

Tells are not the only way you can tip your hand. Being predictable in your betting patterns is just as revealing. If you're too consistent in your play, not only will you know what you're going to do, but so will your opponents!

Poker is a game of deceit. Your actions—checking, betting, calling, and raising—make statements and should create doubts in your opponents' minds. Raises imply strength, but when you do throw extra chips into the pot, you want your opponents to consider the possibility that you might be bluffing. When you call, it often implies weakness, but your opponents should worry about the call being a trap.

One of the worst things a poker player can be is predictable. If your opponents know that you always bet, call, fold, or raise in the same situations, you will be an open book. They will feast upon your chips at the poker table.

If more opponents than usual drop out of the action every time you bet or raise, something may be amiss. You must find that "something" to protect your pots. Whether you have a tell or a predictable betting pattern, you have to adjust your play so you get the proper value for your bets. Your goal is to get maximum value possible out of your hands. When you're strong, you want callers.

If you're pegged as a player who plays only with good hands, or as one who raises every time a good hand is drawn, in no time at all, your opponents will pick up on this habit and adjust their play to take full advantage of the situation. For example, there are aggressive players who tip off good hands by suddenly playing meekly when their cards show strength. This unusual behavior often causes opponents to beware the quiet lion and drop out in marginal situations rather than meet the action.

To some degree, a good player will be predictable, and that is okay. There is always a degree of consistency in good players. But at the same time, there has to be a degree of unpredictability in your play. Part of being a good poker player is varying your play enough so that opponents never know exactly what's up your sleeve.

Betting patterns, particularly in no-limit and pot-limit, are fundamental giveaways of the strength of a player's hand. That is why, in these betting structures, you want to standardize your bets and raises so that your bets aren't revealing extra information to opponents.

WINNING CONCEPT #10:
STRATEGY FOR PLAYING AGAINST A LOOSE PLAYER

Loose players love action. They play too many hands, call too many bets, and stay in pots too long. By playing more hands, they will win more pots, but at the expense of too many bets when they lose. Net result:

overall losses. Since loose players play more hands, their cards will be weaker, on average, than your typical non-loose opponent. So you need to adjust.

When you're in pots against loose players:

1. Call more often at the showdown, since they'll get there with weaker cards.

2. Don't try to move them off of pots when you have nothing. Bluffing just won't work against players who'll call with any hope in their hand.

3. Play more marginal hands than usual when you're heads-up since their average hand strength will be weaker. At the same time, however, stick to a fundamentally solid approach. Don't get drawn into a loose player's game.

Let loose players win their pots. You like to see that. The more they win, the more they have for you to get. When you're in there against them with a big hand, you'll make them pay a hefty price for playing weaker cards to the end against you.

WINNING CONCEPT #11:
STRATEGY FOR PLAYING AGAINST FREQUENT BLUFFERS

Players who bluff often contribute a lot of money to pots. That's good, especially when you're sitting with a better hand than the bluffer. When you draw big hands, if the bluffer is in motion, you're in great shape and can play quietly without revealing the strength of your cards while the pot is built up for you. For example, in games like no-limit hold'em, aggressive bluffers are easy to trap. If you connect, your weak checks and calls encourage the bluffer to pound you right through to the end, allowing you to trap them, sometimes for most of their chips.

Frequent bluffers build chips rapidly, but they'll often see those stacks get halved even faster when better hands connect and take down big pots.

The general strategy against a frequent bluffer is to call his bets more often when you have a hand that can challenge and beat him if he doesn't have the goods. Before calling a bluffer, you must make sure your hand is strong enough on its own merits to make a stand. It must at least have some value to beat any secondary hands the bluffer probably holds.

In other words, don't call a bluffer with a hand that can't beat anything. Just because you know an opponent is bluffing doesn't mean you need to play for the pot. Your hand must stand on its own. Let the bluffer have a lot of the little pots, you'll more than even the score when you take him down for a big one.

WINNING CONCEPT #12:
STRATEGY AGAINST TIGHT PLAYERS

When your opponents are tight, that is, they only enter pots with premium hands, it's time for you to loosen up your game. You should play more aggressively against tight players, since they more readily give up hands. When you bet or raise them, they'll usually fold marginal hands. This means you can easily push them out of pots with any garbage you hold—your cards are irrelevant when an opponent won't defend his hand. If you're playing hold'em, you'll want to consistently attack their blinds, which they won't defend.

You take advantage of tight opponents by always figuring them for a good hand when they're in the pot. Respect their bets; they're generally betting on solid cards. In borderline situations, give tight players the benefit of the doubt and call their bets less often. When you do call their bets, call with cards you figure can win. And if a tight player raises, make sure the pot odds and the strength of your hand justify a call.

Since tight players won't play mediocre hands, you can force them out of the pot early with strong bets. If your hand is mediocre and he bets, give him credit for strength and save your chips.

WINNING CONCEPT #13:
STRATEGY AGAINST PLAYERS WHO DON'T BLUFF

When you're not sure, give the non-bluffer the benefit of the doubt and fold marginal hands. You can save lots of chips against this type of player by calling less with questionable hands and by not having your good hands bluffed out by his scare cards. This type of player is very predictable, and that gives you a big edge when they're at your table.

WINNING CONCEPT #14:
IMPROVE YOUR PLAY BY WATCHING OPPONENTS—AND YOURSELF

Every poker hand is a poker class that can provide a lesson, large or small. Your best teachers are your opponents, and not just the good ones, but the weaker ones as well. You should learn from their good plays and from their mistakes.

You improve your skills at poker by observing and examining every situation and hand to see how it could have been played optimally against a particular opponent or type of opponent. For example, if a player held the absolute best hand, could an extra bet have been forced out of the losers or could more players have been kept in the pot with a different betting pattern? Or on a hand that lost, could it have been played more aggressively so that opponents could have been forced out earlier? Should the player have bowed out earlier himself, realizing that maybe the opponent's betting suggested a better hand than he could beat?

Watch how opponents react to the different situations that come up in a poker game. The more you learn about your fellow players, the better your chances of squeezing extra bets out of them, building bigger pots for yourself when the cards are right, and getting out of the pot when you're hopelessly beat. Hands and situations repeat themselves over and over again in poker. To become a better player, you have to learn from these situations and apply your lessons to future hands.

How well you do in poker is not measured by the actual winning or losing of each hand, but by how well you played that hand. You must always examine your play and ask yourself the question, "Did I play the cards optimally?" Just because you won a hand, it doesn't mean you played it well. Conversely, just because you lost a hand, it doesn't mean you played it poorly. Perhaps you could have won a bigger pot, or perhaps you should have forced out another player and reduced the chances of an opponent getting a lucky draw against you. Maybe you stayed in one card too many. Maybe you shouldn't have played the hand at all.

If you stay aware of how the game is being played and keep track of the tendencies of other players, you can't help but become a better player. And playing better means winning more.

WINNING CONCEPT #15:
IMPROVE YOUR PLAY BY READING BOOKS

There is a tremendous amount of great literature available and every book you read advances your knowledge of the game and gives you more weapons to use at the table. If you play enough hours of poker, you cannot afford not to buy every good book you can get your hands on. Thousands of dollars change hands in one evening of low-limit poker; for the cost of $20 or $30 to get a good book, you are buying an enormous wealth of knowledge. That, by any definition, is a huge bargain.

WINNING CONCEPT #16:
ONLY THE BEST HAND WINS

Do not fall in love with your cards, no matter how pretty they look. There are no prizes for second best at poker. Only the winner takes the cake. If you have kings over sixes on fifth street in seven-card stud, and an opponent gets dealt an open pair of aces, the dirge has begun. If those aces are accompanied by a second pair, you're chasing with a dead hand. Though you may improve, those aces have an equal chance of improving. Unless you have very compelling pot odds, the romantic interlude is over—it's time to fold.

Sometimes you must fold strong hands in the face of heavy betting, even though you suspect that an opponent is bluffing. There's nothing wrong with being bluffed out of pots. That's part of the game. If you are never bluffed out of a pot, that means you're calling too often, and opponents are reaping showdown harvest with your loose play. Good players respect cards and can be bluffed. Only weak players will never give up the ship—until it sinks. Don't worry about trying to scratch out a win in every pot. Just win the ones you can and minimize losses in the ones you can't.

WINNING CONCEPT #17:
EVERY CHIP COUNTS

A poker session is an accumulation of hands won and lost. To come out an overall winner, you must maximize your gains when you win and minimize losses when you lose so that the winnings overshadow the losses and you have a profit to show. One way to shift the balance more in your favor is to avoid throwing chips away in situations you know you shouldn't be playing.

Too often, players toss an "extra chip or two" into a pot, almost as a throwaway or they stay one bet too long in a pot in which they know they're beaten. These bad plays add up to greater losses than players realize. This could be the difference between winning and losing, a big loss and a small loss, or a big win and a small win.

Every chip is valuable. Remember that, and at the end of the night, you'll end up having more chips in your pile. And that's always a good thing.

WINNING CONCEPT #18:
YOU MUST WANT TO WIN

In any sport or pursuit, desire separates the great from the good. Players who really want to win have a hunger that makes them concentrate more, play better, and put in that extra effort that forces good things to happen, or at least lays the groundwork for such conditions. Desire breeds confidence and confidence makes all the difference in the world at the poker table. Confident players get more respect for their bets—opponents fold more often and are less likely to enter pots knowing a confident player may raise up their bets—and make better decisions in key situations.

Players who play without confidence encourage more callers, which means more chances for opponents to draw out and get lucky hands. They also bluff less in situations where that may be the right play. As a result, they win fewer pots by default since opponents are less likely to fold against a player showing little strength.

WINNING CONCEPT #19:
STAY POSITIVE

This concept is closely linked to the concept above. Staying positive about your chances to win breeds confidence and allows you to make the optimal decisions on every hand. Players who grumble about their bad luck and play with negative psychological expectations get less respect on their bets and tend to make poor decisions. They call when they should fold, bet when they should raise, and raise when they should fold.

Keen opponents sense this and step up their own game, becoming even better as an opponent gets worse.

Stay positive, and you'll allow good things to happen at the poker table.

WINNING CONCEPT #20:
VARY YOUR PLAY

In other words, don't be predictable. We've discussed the importance of winning chips, not pots. Obviously, you have to win pots to win chips, but there are different qualities of pots. There are little pots, medium pots, and big pots. Predictable players win smaller pots, unpredictable players get more action and win bigger ones, while the superior players will use leverage to win more than their share of the medium-sized pots.

For example, a rock who only enters the pot with big cards rarely gets good action. All his opponents learn to respect his bets and stay clear of him when he enters the pot. As a result, there are fewer callers and much smaller pots. Loose players, on the other hand, are unpredictable and prone to playing all sorts of hands, leading opponents to widen their choice of hands and play pots for more chips.

Playing optimal poker requires you to find a mix between tight and loose. You want to encourage action, which tight play does not do, but not give chips away as loose play does. There is a saying in poker: action begets action. So you want your opponents to know that you'll gamble with them sometimes so that they'll be drawn into the pot with marginal hands but still feel that they have a shot of winning.

WINNING CONCEPT #21:
BE SMART WITH MONEY MANAGEMENT

It cannot be overstated: smart money management is essential to every player who risks money at the poker table. From betting within one's means to minimizing losses and maximizing gains to emotional control, money management is the core of any winning strategy. Be sure to read the money management chapter carefully and adhere religiously to its advice.

16. PERCEPTIONS & PLAYERS

In this chapter we'll take a look at the human element of the game, the types of players you might face and the perceptions and counter-perceptions that influence the dynamics of a poker game. While you try to determine what kind of hands your opponents may hold, opponents are also evaluating your play, trying to determine the best way to play against you. Understanding what opponents think you're thinking gives you great insight into the best way to play your hand.

Poker is a game where good people skills separate winning players from losing players. It's all about understanding how an opponent will react to any betting action you might make. If you bet, will an opponent call? Will he fold? Will he raise? And when he checks, bets or raises, what is he representing—a strong hand, a weak hand, a monster?

All betting actions are made for particular reasons, and over time, you'll get a better sense of which opponents play aggressively and which won't budge with a bet unless they've got a strong hand. You'll learn which ones stay too long in pots and which ones bluff too often or not at all. You'll start to recognize players who take advantage of late position and others who rarely enter the pot early unless they're strong.

To be successful at poker, you need to know how your cards stack up against your opponents—when you're standing strong, when you're weak, when you're a virtual lock, and when your hand has possibilities but is trailing the hand you've put your opponent on. And while you never really know what opponents hold, you can make educated guesses if you pay attention to the dynamics of the hand—based on the cards you see, betting patterns, positions and actions of active opponents, and the tendencies and styles of players competing for the pot.

Winning players come in a wide variety of flavors, from conservative and methodical to very aggressive, but there is one trait all winning players share in common: people-reading skills. They get a sense of an opponent's tolerance to bets and raises and an idea of when that opponent can be pushed off a pot and when he cannot.

This chapter presents a brief introduction to this complex aspect of poker, hopefully enough to get your thoughts flowing in the right direction.

THE FOUR TYPES OF HANDS

Poker hands can be grouped into four categories of strength: weak, trailing, leading, and monster. Each of these categories represents a situation of perceived strength, because you never know what your opponents hold. At the top end of the spectrum is the **monster** category, which includes hands heavily favored to win the pot. At the bottom end is the **weak** group, which is comprised of hands that are probable losers and rarely worth a bet. The second strongest group are the **leading hands**, cards which appear to be the best at the moment. And then there are the **trailing hands**, cards that probably need improvement to win.

Hand strengths are relative in poker and you always want to get a handle on where you are at in a hand so you can play your cards appropriately. For example, a lowly pair of sevens may take the pot in one hand, while a mighty full house may lose to a higher full house or even a four of a kind in another. Learning to evaluate where you stand is essential for knowing how to proceed with a hand.

We'll start with the category of least strength, the weak hands, and work our way up to the strongest grouping, the monsters.

WEAK HAND STRATEGY

This category of hands is comprised of holdings with no better than longshot chances of improving to winners. These are the worst poker hands, and they have long-term losing expectations. Weak hands should be played only if you can get into a pot cheaply, if you feel that you can muscle opponents off the pot, or if you think you can use superior position to steal blinds or antes.

Otherwise, weak hands should be junked at the first opportunity. When you're a heavy underdog with little hope of winning, you have no business investing your money in the pot. This advice applies to your starting cards, and it applies to your cards if they become weak at any point in the game. It doesn't matter how promising your cards were when they were dealt. Losing hands are losing hands. If you have kings in seven-card stud and an opponent shows aces on board, you're beaten—end of story. Your kings might as well be marshmallows in a rock fight. They're not going to do you any good.

Too many players chase pots with weak hands, hoping for the lucky draw. That kind of strategy is costly and leads to consistent losing sessions. To be an overall winner at poker, you must avoid throwing away money on poor percentage plays.

TRAILING HAND STRATEGY
Trailing hands include hands that do not currently figure to be the best at the moment, nor are they favored to win if the hand is played out to the end; however, they are not big underdogs like the weak hands. This category includes draws to straights and flushes, and

starting hands such as two high cards or a low or medium pair in hold'em—hands which could improve with a good flop.

In general, you want to enter a pot cheaply with a trailing hand or even grab a free card, allowing you to proceed to the next round without cost if all players check. For example, if you're in late position or at a passive table and you're facing just a single bet in a pot that you don't think will be raised, you can enter the pot with less fear.

However, if the cost is two bets, or if you're in early position and vulnerable to raises, trailing hands become chip burners and should be thrown to the wind. The winning possibilities of trailing hands aren't strong enough to warrant investing heavily in a pot.

Position also plays an important role when you have to either bet or fold to enter the pot. From late position, it is safer to enter the pot with a trailing hand because there are few players acting after you. If you're in early position, though, a call would put you in serious danger of being raised after your position. This is not a situation you want with a trailing hand.

Trailing hands have two ways to win. First, the hand can improve to a winner. And second, aggressive betting can force out opponents and win you the pot by default. Sometimes drawing hands are good hands to force the action in a pot as they give you both ways to win.

To sum up, trailing hands are worth a play when the price is right, but if the cost is high, they're rarely worth betting on. Save your sweet dreams for the late night—after the poker game. And save your money as well.

LEADING HAND STRATEGY

This category is comprised of hands that appear likely to win if the hand goes to a showdown, making them favorites or near-favorites. These hands have some strength, but if you don't play them aggressively and force some players out, you allow mediocre hands the chance to draw out and beat you.

The more players in a pot, the greater the average winning hand will be and the higher the chance that a leading hand will become a trailing or weak one. And that is why you want to play aggressively right from the start with leading hands—to either force out the trailing and weak hands, or build up a pot in which you're favored to win. You should never allow opponents to play cheaply. If they want to see the show, they'll have to buy the tickets—at the price of your bets and raises.

As an exercise, deal yourself A-K along with five random hands, then deal out a full board of five cards. Do this twenty times. You'll start seeing that the A-K will win more than the other random hands, but overall, it will suffer more losses than you would expect. Do the same with kings, or aces, and once again, you'll see that these hands suffer against multiple opponents. Repeat this exercise against two opponents or one, and you'll soon see the difference between playing aggressively and narrowing the field—and the wisdom behind it.

As the exercise of dealing out twenty hands with the A-K, K-K and A-A hands amply illustrates, the more weak hands allowed in to see another round of play, the greater the chances are that one of those weaker hands will improve and become a winning hand.

If your leading hand appears to get outdrawn or become less valuable as a hand progresses, reevaluate its strength. Hands are dynamic, getting stronger or weaker as more cards are drawn. If you start with a pocket queens or kings in hold'em, which you figure to be the best hand, and an ace flops, you have to reevaluate where you're at in the deal. Adjust your strategy to the new reality.

To sum up: when you've got a leading hand, you need to protect it by weeding out the competition with aggressive betting. This gives you the best chances of taking down the pot.

MONSTER HAND STRATEGY

Monster hands are big, big hands that are heavily favored to win. They put you in the driver's seat. Barring a very lucky draw by your opponents, you figure to have the best hand at the showdown. Your only strategic concern is how to get as much of your opponents' money in the pot as possible. Ideally, you'd like to be up against one or two opponents with strong, but less powerful hands so that all sorts of chips find their way into the pot.

For example, if you've got Q-Q against two opponents, one with 9-9 and the other with A-K, on a flop of A-Q-9, you're heavily favored to win a huge pot. Even though you would love to raise and reraise until your opponents' pockets are emptied, on a practical level, overzealous betting can drive your opponents out of the pot, which is exactly what you don't want to do when you have a monster. You want action and you have to decide upon the best way to get it. Sometimes that means betting or raising and sometimes it means checking or calling. In no-limit, it could even mean going all-in as a way to set the trap. If conservative betting is an unusual way for you to play a situation, checking or making a weak bet may very well clue in your opponents that you're sandbagging them.

One key strategy for playing monster hands is allowing your opponents to take free cards when necessary so they can catch up. If you get lucky and they catch a good card when they're drawing dead, you've really got them trapped. When you're up against aggressive players, their bets and raises will build the pot while your checks and calls disguise the strength of your hand.

But in all situations, give careful thought on how best to play off your opponents' tendencies to get the maximum amount of money into that pot.

UNDERSTANDING SKILL LEVELS

There are many levels and degrees of skill and aggressiveness among players, but to a great degree, skill levels can be grouped into four general categories: weak and beginning players, average players, superior players, and the very best players.

There will be qualities within the various groups that best describe your own play, though the bottom line measurement in poker is always measured in wins and losses, regardless of how you get there. Or I should say, long term wins and losses. One great session doesn't make a great player just as one terrible session doesn't describe a terrible player. And equally, just because you win in a session doesn't mean you played well, and because you lost, it doesn't mean you played poorly.

Evaluating your skill must be done over a group of sessions. After five playing sessions, you should start getting a feel of how well you're playing in the game you are competing in, though this sample is a little small to make definitive statements. Still, if you're a big loser after five sessions, or a big winner, as a start, this may be a good indication of where you're at in the game. Ten playing sessions, however, is a much better sample. Sometimes players run real good or real bad over a relatively short period of time, but given that there are so many hands played every poker session, be it four or five hours or a marathon of twenty hours or more, this is a more reasonable sample to see how you stack up against the competition you're playing.

When you understand the qualities and skills that describe and separate players between these categories, you'll be able to get insights in how to take your game to the next level.

Let's take a look at the categories now.

WEAK AND BEGINNING PLAYERS

The weak and beginning players play too many hands and stay in pots too long. These players place bet after bet into pots they shouldn't be in because they don't recognize either that they are not getting enough value for their wagers or that they are in a hand in which they are already hopelessly beat. Throwing too many bets into too many pots is a pattern you'll see over and over among weaker players.

Weak and beginning players can also be so conservative that they make little impact on the game. In this group, you can find **rocks**—the tight players who will play only with good cards. The rock's play is so obvious that all opponents without strong enough hands fold at his first sign of activity. But even more prevalent than the rock are the legions of **loose gooses**, players who throw chips at the pot as if they can't get rid of them fast enough.

There are also **action junkies** who play almost every pot. While they'll win more chips than any other player and have some big winning sessions, they will have the worst losing sessions. The action junkie, more than any other player, will be the biggest contributor to other players' bankrolls.

The aggressive beginning and weak players will win more pots than the average player, but with so many of their chips in action with hands that end up losing, they'll find themselves being consistent losers in poker games. On the other hand, the conservative players in this category will barely win any pots and those that are won will be for few chips.

AVERAGE PLAYERS

Average players don't necessarily play too many hands, which right there puts them a notch above the weak and beginning category, but the ones they do enter are played too conservatively. In this category resides the **calling stations**, players who call too many bets (as opposed to raising), and the **rice-and-beans** players, individuals who play simple poker but have no spice to their game. They call when they should be raising, check when they should be betting, and fold when calling or raising might be the better play. In a nutshell, they lack the flair and creativity for the bold move.

Average players play leading hands weakly, allowing opponents to either stay in the pot cheaply for just one bet or to draw free cards. As a result, too many opponents in later position end up drawing out on them. Instead of protecting their hand with aggressive betting, as a strong player would have done, and thinning the competition so they can win a nice pot, the end result is that opponents get "lucky" far too often and put bad beats on them.

While average players play a fundamentally more solid game, they don't recognize situations as well as they could and end up contributing too many bets to other player's pots when they should have been watching from the sidelines. On the other hand, they don't maximize wins from their good hands and get bluffed out on hands they should still be playing. Average players typically lack boldness, which makes them easy to push around. When they do possess the necessary fearless attitude, they pay the price by not folding when they're beat, they'll call big bets in big pots with weaker hands because they suspect bluffing and don't want to give up the pot, when instead, they should have respected the big bets and folded.

Among average players there will still be rocks and gooses, but they'll have more skills than their more novice counterparts. They read situations better and throw away less money. However, better and more aggressive players will still eat them for lunch.

SUPERIOR PLAYERS

The characteristic quality of a superior player is *aggression*. He'll keep firing bets and raises at you, forcing you to make tough decisions. In big bet games like no-limit and pot-limit, aggressive players rule the roost. They consistently take pots away from weak players by leaning on them with bets that don't get called.

PERCEPTIONS & PLAYERS

When aggressive players can push around their opponents, it is a tremendous advantage. And the more aggressive players see that an opponent is unwilling to defend their blinds or their pot, the more bets they'll fire at them and take those pots away. When the conservative player finally plays back, the aggressive player knows the conservative player has the goods and can easily escape big damage by folding against their strength. Advantage: aggressive player.

Unlike average players, who frequently call, superior players will sooner raise than call. In fact, their decision on a play is not usually whether to call or raise, but whether to raise or fold! You'll rarely get a free card out of them. Action will be fiercer, and you'll soon know the meaning of "pay to play." Superior players instill fear in their opponents and leverage every bet to the maximum effectiveness. Opponents tend to think in terms of what the superior player will do anytime he gets involved in a pot, being more worried about his actions, than about those of any other player.

When the situation is right, superior players will punish opponents who have the temerity to bet into their position.

Superior players know how to get out of hands that they're beat in and when to push hard against players who will likely fold. They're great at bluffing, but by the same token, they can be bluffed out of pots themselves.

This category is marked by tough players who have the ability to take over and drive the action at the table. When you're up against superior players, they make you earn every pot against them.

THE VERY BEST

The very best poker players excel in every aspect of the game. They're super aggressive, and they have no fear of any bet thrown their way. They have the uncanny ability to read opponents based on the action and play of the table, and will back that up with big betting when they don't even have the cards to back their bets. This talent allows them to win big pots with hands others would have folded and to play profitable poker at the very highest stakes.

Superstar players like Johnny Chan, Barry Greenstein, Doyle Brunson and the former Chip Reese are so skilled, that given good position, they can beat many players without even looking at their cards—just by reading their opponents' patterns.

17. FIFTEEN ESSENTIAL BLUFFING CONCEPTS

The bluff! The beauty, romance, and drama of poker lies in the bluff. The art of betting aggressively with an inferior hand, one unlikely to win if called, with the intent of causing opponents to fold better hands, is an integral part of poker and a skill that matures with experience.

There are several advantages to bluffing. The first and most obvious advantage is that you can "steal pots" from better hands and win money you otherwise would not have. There is nothing more beautiful than chasing out a better hand and taking the pot for your own. The second advantage to bluffing is that when you're caught, you put doubt in your opponents' minds. They will suspect you for possible garbage every time you contest the pot. This powerful weapon makes your play more difficult to predict, and it will win you bigger pots when you do have strong hands. Players with weaker hands will feel compelled to call your position more often thinking that their hands may be better. While they are keeping you "honest," the pot sizes of your winning hands get larger.

> ## Key Concept
> *Players who are known not to bluff will, on average, win smaller pots than players who are known to bluff.*

Predictable play is costly in poker, whether in the home game, casino game, or club game. Opponents with mediocre hands will know that it is senseless to compete against a player who only bets with strong hands. He's not a bluffer. The result is that the rock does not get as much value on his good hands as he should.

To be successful at poker, bluffing must be an integral part of your game. You'll not only win pots where your hand is not the best one, you'll also win larger pots because opponents will contest your winning hands more often.

I've identified fifteen powerful bluffing concepts that will help you use the powerful weapon of the bluff effectively.

THE FIFTEEN CONCEPTS
1. BLUFFING IN LOW-LIMIT GAMES
In many low-limit games, players simply cannot be chased from a pot. For one, the action is cheap, and the thinking goes, "What's one or two more bets?" For another, low-limit games attract players who can't be chased out of a pot by anything less than an elephant stampede. They'll call bet after bet with terrible hands

in losing situations and hope for the longshot draw that just might give them the winner. They'll get the lucky cards now and then, but in between, their chips will get unmercifully bled from their stacks.

If you're in a low-limit game where players are not getting chased out of pots with maximum bets, there's no point in bluffing. If you can't bluff out an opponent, you need to redirect your strategy toward more basic play, working the cards a little more than working the opponents.

Common wisdom states that you can't ever bluff players out of the pot in low-limit games. That's certainly true for some games, but not for all. You'll find low-limit casino games, say $1-$5 spread-limit, where players respect bets and can be bluffed. After all, to many people, money is money. The stakes may be small, but they would sooner save their bets for situations with better prospects. However, as each game has its own mix of players and particular temperament, you'll see what can and can't be done on a game by game basis.

2. BLUFFING IN MEDIUM TO HIGH LIMIT GAMES

Unlike low-stakes casino games, a bluff in medium to high limit games may resonate from the opening bell right down to the final round. With more money at stake, players are less subject to the friendly game syndrome of staying in the pot "a few more rounds." As you play in higher stake games in cardrooms—where the rule of thumb is that the higher the stakes, the better the level of player—your ability to chase opponents out of the pot will improve. Good players respect bets and can be bluffed; weak players don't understand when their hands can't support heavy betting.

> **Key Concept**
> *The better the player,*
> *the easier it is to run a bluff on him.*

Of course, you have to pick your spots. Every game has its mix of strong and weak players, and you'll need to learn who can be bluffed and who can't. Players who play too many pots are difficult to bluff, as are those that vigorously defend every pot they're in.

But while you won't get the money from these types of players on good bluffing opportunities, as you might from better players, you'll get them for big pots when you have strong hands and they stubbornly won't fold. If you find opponents in your game who can't be bluffed, that's good news anyway. When you get the right trap hand, you've got them set up for a big fall.

Keep in mind this fundamental truth in poker: the better the player, the easier it is to bluff him out of pots, the worse the player, the more he'll call with hands that a better player would fold.

15 ESSENTIAL BLUFFING CONCEPTS

3. SMALL POT VS. LARGE POT BLUFFING

In limit poker, bluffing is more effective in smaller pots than in large pots for the simple reason that, in large pots, there is too much money at stake for players to fold against the cost of a few more bets. With good pot odds and a lot of money at stake, it is hard to force savvy players from the sweet corn in the fields. If an opponent is looking at a 1 in 3 chance of winning, and a bet to play would cost only 1/15 of the pot, it would be foolish not to play. Whether or not opponents have heard the term "pot odds," most players clearly understand the underlying concept—the risk of a small bet is usually worth the reward of a big pot.

Generally speaking, though, bluffs in limit poker are inversely more effective in relation to the size of the pot. Again, risk versus reward. The smaller the pot, the smaller the relative payoff for a single bet; the bigger the pot, the bigger the payoff. In other words, the effectiveness of a bluff is directly correlated to pot odds. If you're faced with calling a bet that is unprofitable in the long run, it is better to fold than to play. This is a mathematical truism.

On the other hand, in big bet poker—no-limit and pot-limit games—you can bluff more effectively in big pots by putting in big bets to take away the odds for drawing hands. This is something you cannot do in limit poker games due to the bet sizes.

4. BLUFF THE RIGHT PLAYER

It's easier to bluff a good player than a weak one, and it's smarter to bluff a player who will likely toss his cards than one who won't. It's stating the obvious, but even so, too many players ignore this simple concept. When considering a bluff, target situations that give you the best chance of success. It's common sense. Many players seem to bluff indiscriminately with no regard for who they're playing against. That is a mistake.

If you get a good scare card in a stud game or on the flop in hold'em, say an ace, don't try to aggressively force out an opponent who will likely call your bluff anyway. What sense would that make? Always choose your situations with potential success in mind. You not only want to play games you can win, but pots you can win. If you can't beat an opponent with a better hand, and can't run him off his hand, just fold.

5. AVOID MULTI-PLAYER BLUFFS

Bluffs are most effective against just one opponent. It's simple math. The more players in the pot, the greater the chances that at least one player will call the bet. Your best bluffs are against just one player and next best are against two. With three or more players in the pot, a bluff will more likely fail because too many opponents are active. With too many opponents, there are too many possibilities that at least one of them will catch good. You can probably expect at least one caller who's got too strong a hand to go out with.

In general, avoid bluffing when more than two players remain in the pot.

6. BLUFF AGAINST "COLD" PLAYERS

When players are in a funk, and can't seem to buy a winning hand, they tend to withdraw into a shell and play more conservatively. If a card dealt in a stud or flop game doesn't help them, they feel it hurts them. Losing feeds on losing and becomes a self-fulfilling prophesy at a poker table. You take advantage of players cursing their bad luck by pushing hard at them when you're in a pot together. Players on a bad roll will fold at the sight of any scare card combined with aggressive betting, thinking, "Here we go again."

7. BLUFF AGAINST SCARED PLAYERS

Players running scared at the table present excellent opportunities for you to take their chips with aggressive play. These are the best players to run bluffs against. This group includes players who have lost heavily and are trying to regain some of their losses, players who have won but are desperately trying to maintain their wins (perhaps they're about to leave and want to exit with profits), players who have lost their confidence, and players generally trying to protect their bank-rolls.

Also, look for players on a downward roll desperately trying to stop their slide, and in a tournament, low-stacked players. Psychologically, you have all these play-ers in a position where they are easily intimidated and thus, less likely to call your aggressive bets and raises. Scared and cautious players are easily bluffed out of pots. The more players worry about their bankroll, the more leverage you have to push them around with aggressive betting and take pots from them. Watch for players who fall into a scared funk during a game and step up your aggression when you can get them into a pot.

8. BLUFF MORE WHEN YOU'RE ON A STREAK

When you're on a hot streak, and winning hands seem to beget winning hands, your opponents will take notice and become less likely to call your bets. It's a natural reaction in poker for opponents to tiptoe around the hot player. When you've got the fear factor going, bluffing becomes a more effective weapon. It's a great time to ride that momentum by playing more hands aggressively and using well-timed bluffs to intimidate opponents. Bud don't overdo the roll, which leads us to the next concept...

9. AVOID OVER-BLUFFING

It is one thing to bluff on occasion and use well-timed plays to drive an opponent off his hand. It is quite another thing to over-bluff. Too many bluffs, and you're not fooling anyone anymore, you're simply playing too loosely. Opponents will quickly catch on to your loose betting, and you'll be sucked into the most expensive pitfall in poker: playing too many hands for too many bets.

15 ESSENTIAL BLUFFING CONCEPTS

Bluffing is most effective in small doses, as a surprise weapon that catches opponents unawares. Use the bluff judiciously, and your success rate with it will be high and profitable.

10. AVOID BLUFFING IN FRIENDLY GAMES

Many poker games, particularly casual home affairs and low-limit cardroom games, tend to be more friendly than competitive. Players stay in more pots and play deeper into the hands. In situations like these, where players want to see more cards before folding and the play is loose, it is difficult to bluff opponents out. Your attempts at bluffing will be fruitless in games where players want to play their hands down to the last card.

Your best strategy in "no fold'em" games is to play a straightforward game, starting with cards that are strong enough to go to the showdown and taking shots with trailing hands which give you the right pot odds.

11. IN BIG-BET GAMES,
BLUFF THE RIGHT AMOUNT

In no-limit and pot-limit games, in which your bets and raises are not regulated to a preset amount as in limit poker, bet-sizing is an art and a science. To be successful at bluffing, you need to push enough chips into the pot to take the odds away from opponents who will enter the pot cheaply if they are allowed to.

For example, if there is $500 in the pot and you bet only $100, it is easy for most players to call this bet. You're making it profitable for them. So where's the bluff? And if you make it cheap for players to take a shot with drawing hands and they hit, their hands can be disguised and they can win big, big pots if you keep pushing at them.

If you want opponents out of a pot, you have to make the bet meaningful. You have to give them a reason to muck their cards. In big bet games, this usually means a pot-sized bet. Continuing with our example above, if there is $500 in the pot, make your bet at least $500, not $100, and that will give your opponents more reason to think about folding their cards than playing them. The greater the risk, the greater the fear an opponent has in playing his hand, and the more likely your big bet will work for the intended purpose.

12. TOURNAMENT BLUFFING

Tournaments are all about survival. So when you have opponents who are low-stacked and protecting their chips, your bluffs become powerful and highly successful weapons. You can steal their blinds and force them out of pots with aggressive betting and raising much more effectively than opponents who have ample chips.

Late position blind and ante stealing becomes more important the deeper into a tournament you go. Look for players who won't defend their blinds or pots and put the pressure on them. Look especially for players who are unwilling to take chances; they're the easiest to take chips from.

13. ONLINE BLUFFING

There is a tendency for online players in limit games to play more hands and call down opponents to the river, so you'll want to bluff less. Obviously, many of the tells you use to read players in live games are useless online, however, the power of bets speak strongly in any poker game, live or on the Internet. In big-bet games, bluffing can be more effective, but again, the tendency of online players to call more often must be factored in when choosing situations to make a play.

14. BLUFF BY POSITION

In the first round of betting, the more opponents you have to go through, the more likely it is that a player behind you will be dealt cards good enough to call or raise. Your best raising positions are on the button and the cutoff seat that acts just before the button. These are the positions from which most of the bluffing occurs.

In no-limit and pot-limit games, a raise coming into the pot from an early position is sometimes effective under the right circumstances since opponents give more respect to early position raises (which suggest strength) than late ones (which suggest steals). This is especially true if you've been playing tight. But keep in mind that early position bluffs are best used sparingly and only under the right circumstances, for the obvious reason that, if you get reraised and hold garbage, you'll probably have to release your cards along with the extra chips you've already put into the pot.

15. SITUATIONAL BLUFFING

If you've bet forcefully with your starting cards, especially in no-limit and pot-limit, the next betting round is an opportunity to continue betting hard and induce your opponent to fold—even if your hand has little value and especially when opponents miss the flop, which will often happen. For example, in hold'em, when you've represented strength preflop and continue betting on the flop, it is difficult for opponents to call unless they've connected with the flop.

18. CARDROOM POKER

Cardroom poker is different than poker played in your regular Friday night game. The level of play may be superior to what you are accustomed to, and once you get to stakes of $10/$20 limits, some of the players you will be competing against will be low-level professionals who make a living at the game. Unlike your poker-playing buddies back home, players at these games are a lot less concerned about how your week went and a lot more interested in whatever green you're holding that they hope to move into their own pile.

Going against local pros at smaller stakes games doesn't mean you can't win money, it just means you need to play better and be a better player. To win money, you don't have to be the best player at your table, you just need to be better than some of the other players. There are always suckers at every game, patsies who never seem to get better and are consistent losers contributing to everybody's pots. And in a popular casino setting, there will be always be plenty of tourists whose skills will vary from pretty good to not very good at all. So there are plenty of opportunities for you to walk away from the table with more chips than you started with.

I used a $10/$20 game above as an example of a cutoff point for a reason. And this is why: the level of money being wagered in a public poker game has everything to do with the average level of competition you'll be playing against—and thus, your chances of winning.

Let's look at that concept now.

STAKES AND COMPETITION LEVEL

In cardrooms, there is a simple truth: the larger the stakes, the better the players. Pros playing in the $5/$10 game compete there because they're not good enough, gutsy enough, or well-financed enough to play at say, the $15/$30 game. The same applies for the $15/$30 and higher games. To some degree, you can measure a pro's skills by the betting level of game he plays. Players that squeeze out profits at $5/$10 will get picked clean at $15/$30, while $15/$30 players will get chewed up and spit out at $30/$60. If players could afford to profitably play for bigger stakes, they would move up to the bigger fish pond.

As a poker player, no matter how small or large your bankroll, you should gauge your skill level in relation to the level of game being played. If you're running over a game or at least holding your own, you can consider moving up to higher stakes. However, if the game is running over you, then you're not ready to compete against a bigger money game. All you'll do there is take a worse whipping.

CARDROOM POKER

As you move up the money tree and play higher stakes games, you'll be running with bigger wolves, so you want to make sure your skill level is high enough to compete. And the best way to judge that is by your results: did you lose money or did you win money?

19. PLAYING POKER PROFESSIONALLY

In this chapter, I'm going to give you a brief look at the realities of playing professional poker. While you can make money at poker—and should if you follow the advice in this book—playing at a professional level is a much, much different can of wax.

THE COLD REALITIES

The reality of playing poker professionally may shock you. And while it may not make sense at first glance, if you ask around, you'll start understanding that there is plenty of truth in the sobering statement that follows: about 95% of poker players are overall losers! And of the few who do succeed at the game, a large percentage of these players give their poker winnings right back to the craps tables or the sports bookies.

So what gives? Why don't more than a few players make money playing poker in cardrooms, even though it is a skill-based game?

First, the vast majority of poker players compete at lower level games, $10/$20 stakes and under. Now, while many of these players consistently beat the other players, they don't necessarily beat the game. Or at least not enough to make the game worthwhile. How's that make sense? It's all about the rake or the time collection fees. The rakes pulled out of pots by the house in low-limit games are too high a percentage for many players to overcome if they want to make a living that includes some sort of lifestyle beyond the basics.

THE SECOND INCOME: PROVE YOU CAN WIN

So before I go any further into this discussion, throw away any thoughts you have of earning your primary source of income through poker until you can earn enough money playing poker as a secondary source of income. Because, if you can't earn enough on the side, you have little chance of making professional poker work as a full-time endeavor. Now, let's continue.

MORE REALITIES

To play professional poker requires that you meet all three of the following requirements:

1. You have to be able to beat the competition at the game you play. Let's assume you do a pretty good job at that. So...

2. You have to overcome the cost of the rake and the dealer tips, a double taxation that impedes your ability to come out ahead. And finally...

3. You need to earn enough money to pay rent, buy groceries, and maybe take care of your family—the sort of stuff that money does.

These last two requirements cannot be met at a $3/$6 or $5/$10 cardroom poker game.

If you live on your own with minimal expenses, you may be able to scrape by at a $10/$20 game. However, if subsistence living or slightly better than that is not your thing, or if you have some real expenses and desires for a higher quality life, you have no chance to make it at $10/$20 games. There just isn't enough money at the game. So you need to move up in limits. But as you move up in limits, the players get tougher and you begin competing against poker players who have the same aspirations as you. Which means you need to play really good poker.

The $15/$30 game is really the lowest limit you can hope to attack the game on a professional level. At these stakes, the percentage of rake you lose to the house is moderate and easy to overcome, and if you can outplay your fellow players, you can start making some serious money. If is the operative word. As discussed above, this is something you'll need to prove to yourself first, before making any life-altering decisions.

OTHER FACTORS

There is a lot more to being a professional than just being able to win money at a $15/$30 or higher poker game. You also need enough of a bankroll to handle the inevitable ups and downs in the game and equally important, you need the right mental make-up to handle these swings. You will encounter losing streaks that will test your bankroll and your ability to mentally withstand losing money, especially with the pressure of knowing you have to win money. And at the same time, this bankroll must be enough to pay the bills.

This is a lot of pressure for the average person and not many people are cut out to handle this kind of stress. The paychecks are uncertain and weeks, perhaps even a month or two, will pass in which bad losses are sustained. If a player is not cut out for this or cannot afford a lack of income over a month or two, or worse, actual losses to the bankroll, then a losing streak can make a player press and change his game. And that is what almost always occurs.

Altering a solid game plan would be the death toll for a player who is not mentally equipped to handle the emotional and financial rigors of taking a bad hit.

To win on a serious level, you must be able to lose on a serious level—and stay balanced. It's always easy when you're winning. What you're made of will come out when the chips are down. If your game stays the same, you've got a shot. If losing changes your game, the conclusion is predictable and not favorable. Put it this way: if it were easy, everyone would be doing it.

LAST WORD ON PLAYING PROFESSIONALLY

Can you make money playing smart poker? Absolutely! However, playing professionally, as I'm trying to impress upon you, is not easy and not for everyone. Play smart and go step-by-step. If you're a casual player, keep yourself in a comfort zone where you walk into games with the expectation to win.

And if you aspire to go professional, it's the same deal. Step-by-step and you'll see what happens.

20. MONEY MANAGEMENT

To be a winner at any form of gambling, including poker, you must exercise sound money management principles and have emotional control. The temptation to ride a winning streak too hard in the hopes of making a big killing or to bet wildly during a losing streak, trying for a quick comeback, are the most common factors that destroy gamblers. Inevitably, big winning sessions dissipate into small wins or disastrous setbacks, while moderately bad losing sessions can turn into nightmares.

In every gambling pursuit, luck plays a role and fluctuations in one's fortunes are common. Your ability to successfully deal with these swings is a vital element in the winning formula. Luck certainly plays a role in what cards are drawn, and, in the short run, can sway its weight toward or against you. However, the overriding factor in poker is skill. It is how you play your cards that determines whether you'll be a winner or a loser.

Good players don't always win, just as poor players don't always lose. That's a fact of life at the poker tables.

You can't win every hand or every session. However, if you stick by the winning principles outlined in this book and follow the money management advice outlined in this chapter, you should end up a consistent winner at poker.

An integral part of the winning formula is exercising self-control. If you consistently give your winnings back to your opponents, you don't have a chance to win. In a sense, you'll be a player who refuses to win. No matter how well a poker session is going, if you feel the need to keep playing until your chips are gone, you need to reexamine your motivations and psychology, because you've either subconsciously taken on losing habits or are playing beyond a timeframe in which you have the winning edge.

To be a winner, you must play with the percentages, not against them. You cannot take on the mindset of a bettor who plays as if the goal were to lose his money. If that player can't lose it all today, there's always tomorrow. For players hell-bent on losing—and there are many players like this—it doesn't take long for losses to catch up with them. We've all seen it happen time and time again.

But losing is not what this book is about. It's about winning, and that's where I want your focus to be. What I'm trying to teach you here is how to win and how to think like a winner. Part of this formula is having the desire to win. Part is using the winning techniques and strategies I describe throughout this book. Another part—the most important part—is managing your money properly. If you don't handle your money intelligently and with a good plan from the start, you're going to be a loser at gambling.

How you feel most definitely affects your overall chances of winning. There's no question about that. A gambler who goes into a game with the goal of winning does everything he can to achieve that goal. This player will closely follow the money management advice in this section. He'll play within his means, set reasonable limits, and control himself at the table. When he's winning big, he'll make sure a good chunk of that money stays with him.

Smart money management requires you to have a bankroll large enough to withstand the normal fluctuations of a poker game and to play for stakes within your financial and emotional means. In a sense, you must be street smart. There's no worse mistake than playing with money that you need for rent, food, or other living expenses. Your constant fear of losing that money will affect your play and influence you to make decisions that run contrary to sound poker principles. This brings us to the most important gambling dictum.

> *Never gamble with money*
> *you cannot afford to lose,*
> *either financially or emotionally.*

This essential principle cannot be emphasized enough. Putting money you need at risk is foolish. Poker involves chance and the short term possibilities of taking a loss are real, no matter how easy the game may appear to be and no matter how stacked the odds are. Unexpected streaks occur in poker and if you haven't prepared for the eventuality that they happen, you could be left short and in trouble. If you never play over your head, you'll never suffer.

Find a game with stakes that make you comfortable, a game where the betting range fits your temperament and emotional makeup. If the larger bets of the particular game you're playing make your heart pump too hard, you're in over your head. You need to find a game offering lower betting limits.

When you play with "scared money," you're easily bullied and pushed away from your optimum playing style. To win, you must go into the action with a mental edge and with every emotional asset you have. You must not give your opponents the chance to push you around because the stakes are too dear for you. If you do, your opponents will figure that out quickly, and you'll be at a disadvantage you will be unable to overcome. You'll be very easy pickings.

Remember that poker is a form of entertainment. As such, you must keep it in perspective. If the fear of losing money creates undue anxiety for you, the entertainment value (and probably your winning expectation) will slip rapidly. It's time to take a breather. Recoup your confidence then hit the tables with fresh vigor. Play only with that winning feeling. Recognizing that emotions affect the quality of play is an important step in making poker an enjoyable and profitable experience.

BANKROLLING

There are two types of bankroll requirements you should have available for your poker endeavors: table bankroll and total bankroll. **Table bankroll** is the amount of money you bring to the table and risk losing in any one session. **Total bankroll** is the amount of money you have available to help you weather the inevitable losing streaks that occur in any form of gambling while still having enough funds to play pressure-free poker.

Let's look at each one in turn.

TABLE BANKROLL

As a rule of thumb, you'll want your table bankroll to be thirty times the maximum or big bet in a limit game for a sufficient table stake. For example, if you're playing a $5/$10 game, buy in for $300 ($10 x 30). Similarly, at a $1-$4 spread-limit game, you'll want $120 ($4 x 30) and for a $10/$20 game, $600 ($20 x 30). In no-limit and pot-limit games, you'll want a bigger buy-in because the fluctuation will be much greater. You generally want enough of a bankroll so that you're not at a money disadvantage to your opponents, but in no case should you have less than three times the minimum buy-in for the game, with five times that amount giving you more breathing room for some bad streaks. And if you lose that, your confidence may go with it, so you may want to call it a day.

TOTAL BANKROLL

If you casually play poker with friends once a week, or in cardrooms as a recreational activity, you don't need to be so concerned about a total poker bankroll, just what you're willing to risk in that one game. You can look at it as an allowance that you have for gambling.

However, if you plan on playing poker on a serious, semi-professional, or professional level, you need to have enough money to sustain the normal fluctuations common to any gambling pursuit. You'll want that total bankroll to be at least 300 times the size of the big bet to be properly financed in limit games. For example, in a $5/$10 game, you'll want a total bankroll of $3,000, and if you're playing $10/$20, you'll need double that amount, $6,000.

If you're playing pot-limit or no-limit poker, you'll want more like 500 times the size of the big blind or big bet, whichever is appropriate to the game, to handle the greater volatility of those betting structures.

These bankroll requirements will give you enough breathing room to withstand losing streaks and still have enough money to come back and play pressure-free poker.

MONEY MANAGEMENT

KNOWING WHEN TO QUIT

What often separates the winners from the losers is that the winners leave the table as winners, and when they're losing, they restrict their losses to affordable amounts. Smart players never allow themselves to be wiped out in one session. It is important to limit your single session table stake to the limits mentioned above. If you do not dig in for more money, you can never be a big loser. You can't always win, that's the reality of a poker game. Take a break and play again when you're fresh and brimming with confidence.

You won't always be at the top of your game, no player maintains his best level of play every day or even every minute at the table. You may be exhausted after hours of play, annoyed with another player, or simply frustrated by bad hands. Whatever the case may be, it is important to realize that anytime you lose your concentration, it will hurt your play and your profit potential will suffer as a result. When this occurs, it is time to take a break.

You might even find yourself in a game where everything's going your way. You're winning big, but you're getting tired. You feel like a superior player, but you've started making mistakes. You hate to leave such a choice table. What should you do? Leave. Once you start making mistakes, you lose your edge. It won't be long before you start handing back your winnings. Of course, it's tough to leave a game you feel is ripe for your skills, but when the edge is gone, it's gone.

When you can no longer take full advantage of a ripe opportunity, end your playing session and take your winnings home with you.

IS A POKER GAME EVER THAT GOOD?

You might hear pros talk about the concept that if a game is good, you shouldn't cash out, regardless of how bad your session is going. But that is incorrect. It is essential that you establish stop-loss limits in any one session and stick to them.

First, you don't want to get beaten so badly in one session that you are demoralized and feel pressure to dig yourself out of a hole which is so big that it seems you can't do so without taking bigger risks and putting yourself in jeopardy of a much worse situation. That is an invitation to big trouble. Second, at a certain point, losses erode confidence and when you don't have confidence, the animal instinct takes over and the wolves at your table will smell the weakness and will eat you alive. Third, face it, it's not your day. You're either playing badly, or luck is so bad, that it will make you play badly worrying about it.

Even if you think the game is good, when you're losing, imagine what your opponents are thinking!

MAXIMIZE WINS/MINIMIZE LOSSES

If you play poker regularly and your goal is to win money on a consistent basis, you must not see every session as an end in itself and try to force wins when they just may not be there. Again, you can't win every time. During the times you lose, restrict your losses to a reasonable amount. You can't win every session, but if you're good, you can win most of them. Just as it's important to maximize your winnings at every winning session, it's equally important to minimize your losses at the losing ones.

Professional poker players have a saying: life is one long poker game. This means you can't judge your results by a hand, a few hands or even a few sessions. The game is not "over" because you walk from the table. There will be another day and another game. Play your cards right, and you'll get your day.

21. LAST WORDS

We've covered a lot of material in this book. Hopefully, I've provided some insights that you can use like alchemy to turn cards into gold at the poker tables. You can't control the cards you get at poker, but you can control how you play them. One session or a few sessions can deal you some bad luck, but overall, your destiny at the poker table is in your hands. If you play well, the winnings will come.

You can be a winner at poker and make money consistently. But it requires solid effort, some thought, and a desire to win. All else being equal, as with everything in life, the individual with desire has a tremendous advantage over the player who does not.

Play smart and make it your goal to get better every game. Learn from your opponents, learn from the situations you face, and learn by buying more books and devouring the information. And always be smart with your money and your emotions. That, above all, is the best advice I can give you in this book.

I'll see you at the tables. Good skill!

GLOSSARY

Ace: The card with one spot. The highest ranking card in high poker; in lowball, the lowest and therefore most valuable card.

Act: To bet, raise, fold, or check.

Active Player: Player still in competition for the pot.

Add-on: Chips purchased by adding on, or the cost of those chips.

Add-on tournament: A tournament that allows players a final purchase of a specified amount of additional chips, usually at the end of the first few rounds of play.

Ante: Mandatory bet placed into the pot by players before the cards are dealt.

Ante-up: A call for a player or players to put their antes into the pot.

Bet: Money wagered and placed into the pot.

Bicycle: In lowball, the A-2-3-4-5—the best possible hand. Also called the **Wheel**.

Big Blind: The larger of two mandatory bets made by the player two seats to the left of the dealer button position.

Blind: A mandatory bet made on the first round of betting. Also, the player making that bet.

Blind Bet: The blind bet itself. Also, a bet placed without looking at one's cards.

Blinded Out: Having lost all one's chips, or a majority of them, to the forced antes and blind bets, without playing hands.

Bluff: To bet or raise with an inferior hand for the purpose of intimidating opponents into folding their cards and making the bluffer a winner by default.

Board: The face-up cards shared by all players. Also **Community Cards**.

Bonus: Optional rule where a set amount is paid by all players to any holder of a high ranking hand such as a straight flush or a royal flush. Also called a **Royalty**.

Bring-In: Forced opening bet in seven-card stud, or the amount required to open betting.

Button: The player occupying the dealer position who goes last in all rounds except the preflop; the disk used to indicate this position.

Buy-In: A player's investment of chips in a poker game or the actual amount of cash he uses to "buy" chips for play.

Call: To bet an amount equal to a previous bet on a current round of betting. Also known as **Calling a Bet** or **Seeing a Bet**.

Cap: Limit to the number of raises allowed in a betting round.

Cash Game: A game played for real money; a non-tournament game.

Check: The act of "not betting" and passing the bet option to the next player while still remaining an active player.

Check and Raise: A player's raising of a bet after already checking in that round.

Community Cards: The face-up cards shared by all players. Also **Board**.

Cut: The amount of money taken from the pot by the house as its fee for running the game, also called **House Cut**, **Vigorish**, and the **Rake**; the act of separating the cards into two piles and restacking them in reverse order.

Dealer: The player or casino employee who shuffles the cards and deals them out to the players.

GLOSSARY

Dealer's Choice: A rule where the current dealer chooses the poker variation to be played.

Deuce: A card term for the 2 of any suit.

Down: A card dealt with its pips "face-down" so that its value is known only to the holder of the card. Cards that are dealt face-down are called **Downcards** or **Closed Cards**.

Draw: The exchange of cards allowed after the first round of betting in draw poker variations.

Draw Out: The evolution of an inferior hand into a good one by the drawing of advantageous cards.

Draw Poker: A form of poker where all cards are dealt "closed," and seen only by their holder.

8-or-Better: In high-low poker, a requirement that a player must have five unpaired cards of 8 or less to qualify for the low end of the pot.

Face: The side of a card exposing its value.

Face Card: Any jack, queen, or king. Also **Picture Card**.

Face Down: A card positioned such that its rank and suit faces the table and cannot be viewed by competing players. Cards dealt this way are also known as **Downcards**.

Face Up: A card positioned such that its rank and suit faces up and is therefore visible to all players. Cards dealt this way are also known as **Upcards** or **Open Cards**.

Fifth Street: The fifth card received in seven-card stud; the last round of betting in hold'em and Omaha.

Flop: In hold'em and Omaha, the first three cards simultaneously dealt face-up for communal use by all active players.

Flush: A hand of five cards of the same suit.

Flush Draw: Three or four cards of one suit needing one or two more cards of that suit, respectively, to complete a flush

Fold: Get rid of one's cards, thereby becoming inactive in the current hand and ineligible to play for the pot.

Four-Flush: A hand of four cards of the same suit.

Four of a Kind: A hand containing four cards of identical value, such as K-K-K-K (four kings).

Four-Straight: A hand containing four cards in numerical sequence, such as 7-8-9-10.

Fourth Street: Fourth card dealt in seven-card stud; fourth community card exposed in hold'em.

Free Card: A betting round where all players checked, thereby allowing players to proceed to the next round of play without cost. Also called a **Free Ride**.

Freeze-out (tournament or game): A tournament or game played until one player has all the chips.

Full House: A hand consisting of three of a kind and a pair, such as 7-7-7-K-K.

Hand: The cards a player holds; the best five cards a player can present.

Head-to-Head: Hand or game played by two players only, one against the other. Also **Heads-Up**.

High-low: Poker variation in which players compete for the best high and low hands, with the winner of each getting half the pot.

High Poker: Poker variations in which the highest hand wins.

Holecard: Card held by a player whose value is hidden from other players.

Joker: The "53rd" card in a deck bearing the drawing of a joker or clown; sometimes used as a wild card.

Kicker: Unmatched side card, usually referring to a pair.

Level: See Round.

Limit Poker: Betting structure in which the minimum and maximum bet sizes are set at fixed amounts, usually in a two-tiered structure such as $5/$10.

Limp: Call a bet as a way to enter the pot cheaply.

GLOSSARY

Live Card: Card that is not out of play and is still available to be drawn.

Low Poker: A form of poker in which the lowest hand wins.

Main Pot: When a player is all in and two or more competing players still have chips, the original pot containing the matched bets and raises of all players, as opposed to side pot.

Misdeal: A deal deemed illegal and therefore invalid.

No-Limit: Betting structure in which the maximum bet allowed is limited only by the amount of money the bettor has on the table.

Nuts: The best hand possible given the cards on board.

One Pair: Hand containing two cards of the same rank, such as Q-Q or 7-7.

Opener: The player making the first bet in a betting round; the bet itself.

Openers: In jacks or better, hands that can open the betting (consisting of a pair of jacks or higher ranking hands).

Overcard: A holecard higher in rank than any board card. For example, a jack is an overcard to a flop of 10-6-2.

Pat Hand: In draw poker, a hand to which no cards are drawn; also implies an excellent hand.

Picture Card: The jack, queen, or king.

Pocket Cards: In hold'em and Omaha, the two face-down cards received by all players.

Position: A player's relative position to the player acting first in a poker round.

Pot: The sum total of all antes and bets placed in the center of the table by players during a poker hand and collected by the winner or winners of that hand.

Pot-Limit: Betting structure in which the largest bet can be no more than the current size of the pot.

Pot Odds: A concept which examines the cost of a bet against the money to be made by winning the pot and compares this to a player's chances of winning that pot.

Preflop: The first betting round in hold'em, when each player has only his two pocket cards.

Premium Starting Hands: One in a group of the best starting cards.

Quads: Four of a kind.

Qualifier: In high-low games, a requirement that a player must have five unpaired cards of 8 or less to win the low end of the pot.

Raise: A wager that increases a previous bet.

Rake: The amount of money taken out of the pot by the house as its fee for running the game.

Rebuy: The purchase of more chips. Often specifically such purchase in a rebuy tournament.

Rebuy Period: In a rebuy tournament, the period of time—usually the first three rounds—during which players can buy additional chips if they fall below a specified total.

Rebuy Tournament: A tournament that allows players to buy more chips when they lose all their current ones, an option usually restricted to the first three levels of play.

Reraise: A bet equaling a previous bet and raise, plus an additional bet—a raise of a raise.

Ring Game: A cash game with a full table of players, usually seven or more.

River: The fifth community card on board.

Rough: In lowball, backing cards that are relatively high, such as 8-7-5-4-3, a rough 8.

Round: In a tournament, a fixed period of play that ends with increased blinds or antes or both. Also **level**. The complete cycle of checks, bets, folds, and raises occurring after each new card or cards are dealt.

GLOSSARY

Royal Flush: An A-K-Q-J-10 of the same suit. The highest ranking hand in high poker.

Scoop: In a high-low game, win both the high and low ends of a pot.

Set: Three of a kind.

Seventh Street: The seventh and final card dealt in seven-card stud.

Shorthanded: A poker game played with six players or less.

Showdown: The final act of a poker game, where remaining players reveal their hands to determine the winner of the pot.

Side Pot: When one player has bet all his chips and two or more opponents remain, a segregated pot created that can only be won by players who still have chips to bet.

Sixth Street: The sixth card dealt in seven-card stud.

Small Blind: The smaller of two mandatory bets made by the player sitting immediately to the left of the dealer button position.

Smooth: In lowball, backing cards that are relatively low, such as 8-4-3-2-A, a smooth 8.

Stand Pat: In draw poker, to draw no cards.

Standard Raise: In no-limit and pot-limit, a raise of three times the size of the big blind.

Steal: Bet or raise with an inferior hand that would probably lose if played to the showdown, with the goal of forcing opponents to fold so that the pot can be won by default.

Steal the Blinds: On the first round of betting, bluff opponents out of a pot no one has entered so that the blinds can be won without a fight.

Straight: A sequence of five consecutive cards of mixed suits, such as 4-5-6-7-8.

Straight Flush: A sequence of five consecutive cards in the same suit, such as 8-9-10-J-Q of spades.

Stud Poker: Variation of poker where one or more cards are visible to the other players.

Suited: Cards of the same suit.

Table Stakes: A rule stating that a player's bet or call of a bet is limited to the amount of money he has on the table in front of him.

Tell: An inadvertent mannerism or reaction that reveals information about a player's hand.

Third Street: The first round of betting in seven-card stud.

Three of a Kind: Poker hand containing three cards of the same rank, such as 4-4-4.

Tournament: A competition among players who start with an equal number of chips and play until one player holds all the chips. Players compete for prizes, typically cash, and get eliminated when they run out of chips.

Tournament Chips: Chips used only for tournaments and that have no cash value.

Trips: Three of a kind. Also **Set**.

Turn: The fourth community card on board.

Two Pair: Poker hand containing two sets of two cards of the same rank, such as J-J-5-5.

Two-Way Hand: A hand that can be played for both high and low.

Under the Gun: The first player to act in a betting round.

Units: Bet size used as a standard measurement.

Up: A card dealt with its pips "face-up" so that its value can be viewed by all players. Cards that are dealt face-up are called **Upcard**s.

Wild Cards: Cards designated as "wild" can be given any value, even as a duplicate of a card already held.

WPT: World Poker Tour.

WSOP: World Series of Poker.

GREAT CARDOZA POKER BOOKS
ADD THESE TO YOUR LIBRARY - ORDER NOW!

THE POKER TOURNAMENT FORMULA *by Arnold Snyder.* Start making money now in fast no-limit hold'em tournaments with these radical and never-before-published concepts and secrets for beating tournaments. You'll learn why cards don't matter as much as the dynamics of a tournament—your position, the size of your chip stack, who your opponents are, and above all, the structure. Poker tournaments offer one of the richest opportunities to come along in decades. Every so often, a book comes along that changes the way players attack a game and provides them with a big advantage over opponents. Gambling legend Arnold Snyder has written such a book. 368 pages, $19.95.

POKER TOURNAMENT FORMULA 2: Advanced Strategies for Big Money Tournaments *by Arnold Snyder.* Probably the greatest tournament poker book ever written, and the most controversial in the last decade, Snyder's revolutionary work debunks commonly (and falsely) held beliefs. Snyder reveals the power of chip utility—the real secret behind winning tournaments—and covers utility ranks, tournament structures, small- and long-ball strategies, patience factors, the impact of structures, crushing the Harringbots and other player types, tournament phases, and much more. Includes big sections on Tools, Strategies, and Tournament Phases. A must buy! 496 pages, $24.95.

CRASH COURSE IN BEATING TEXAS HOLD'EM *by Avery Cardoza.* Perfect for beginning and somewhat experienced players who want to jump right in on the action and play cash games, local tournaments, online poker, and the big televised tournaments where millions of dollars can be made. Both limit and no-limit hold'em games are covered along with the essential strategies needed to play profitably on the preflop, flop, turn, and river. The good news is that you don't need to memorize hands or be burdened by math to be a winner—just play by the no-nonsense basic principles outlined here. 208 pages, $14.95

POKER TALK: Learn How to Talk Poker Like a Pro *by Avery Cardoza.* This fascinating and fabulous collection of colorful poker words, phrases, and poker-speak features more than 2,000 definitions. No longer is it enough to know how to walk the walk in poker, you need to know how to talk the talk! Learn what it means to go all in on a rainbow flop with pocket rockets and get it cracked by cowboys, put a bad beat on a calling station, and go over the top of a producer fishing with a gutshot to win a big dime. You'll soon have those railbirds wondering what *you* are talking about. 304 pages, $9.95.

OMAHA HIGH-LOW: Play to Win with the Odds *by Bill Boston.* Selecting the right hands to play is the most important decision to make in Omaha. This is the *only* book that shows you the chances that every one of the 5,278 Omaha high-low hands has of winning the high end of the pot, the low end of it, and how often it is expected to scoop all the chips. You get all the vital tools needed to make critical preflop decisions based on the results of more than 500 million computerized hand simulations. You'll learn the 100 most profitable starting cards, trap hands to avoid, 49 worst hands, 30 ace-less hands you can play for profit, and the three bandit cards you must know to avoid losing hands. 248 pages, $19.95.

HOW TO BEAT SIT-AND-GO POKER TOURNAMENTS by Neil Timothy. There is a lot of dead money up for grabs in the lower limit sit-and-gos and Neil Timothy shows you how to go and get it. The author, a professional player, shows you how to reach the last six places of lower limit sit-and-go tournaments four out of five times and then how to get in the money 25-35 percent of the time using his powerful, proven strategies. This book can turn a losing sit-and-go player into a winner, and a winner into a bigger winner. Also effective for the early and middle stages of one-table satellites. 176 pages, $14.95.

DOYLE BRUNSON'S EXCITING BOOKS
ADD THESE TO YOUR COLLECTION - ORDER NOW!

SUPER SYSTEM *by Doyle Brunson.* This classic book is considered by the pros to be the best book ever written on poker! Jam-packed with advanced strategies, theories, tactics and money-making techniques, no serious poker player can afford to be without this hard-hitting information. Includes fifty pages of the most precise poker statistics ever published. Features chapters written by poker's biggest superstars, such as Dave Sklansky, Mike Caro, Chip Reese, Joey Hawthorne, Bobby Baldwin, and Doyle. Essential strategies, advanced play, and no-nonsense winning advice on making money at 7-card stud (razz, high-low split, cards speak, and declare), draw poker, lowball, and hold'em (limit and no-limit). This is a must-read for any serious poker player. 628 pages, $29.95.

SUPER SYSTEM 2 *by Doyle Brunson.* SS2 expands upon the original with more games and professional secrets from the best in the world. New revision includes Phil Hellmuth Jr. along with superstar contributors Daniel Negreanu, winner of multiple WSOP gold bracelets and 2004 Poker Player of the Year; Lyle Berman, 3-time WSOP gold bracelet winner, founder of the World Poker Tour, and super-high stakes cash player; Bobby Baldwin, 1978 World Champion; Johnny Chan, 2-time World Champion and 10-time WSOP bracelet winner; Mike Caro, poker's greatest researcher, theorist, and instructor; Jennifer Harman, the world's top female player and one of ten best overall; Todd Brunson, winner of more than 20 tournaments; and Crandell Addington, no-limit hold'em legend. 704 pgs, $29.95.

CARO'S GUIDE TO DOYLE BRUNSON'S SUPER SYSTEM *by Mike Caro.* Working with World Champion Doyle Brunson, the legendary Mike Caro has created a fresh look to the "Bible" of all poker books, adding new and personal insights that help you understand the original work. Caro breaks 36 concepts into either "Analysis, Commentary, Concept, Mission, Play-By-Play, Psychology, Statistics, Story, or Strategy. Lots of illustrations and winning concepts give even more value to this great work. 86 pages, 8 1/2 x 11, $19.95.

ACCORDING TO DOYLE *by Doyle Brunson.* Learn what it takes to be a great poker player by climbing inside the mind of poker's most famous champion. Fascinating anecdotes and adventures from Doyle's early career playing poker in roadhouses are interspersed with lessons from the champion who has made more money at poker than anyone else in history. Learn what makes a great player tick, how he approaches the game, and receive candid, powerful advice from the legend himself. 208 pages, $14.95.

MY 50 MOST MEMORABLE HANDS *by Doyle Brunson.* This instant classic relives the most incredible hands by the greatest poker player of all time. Great players, legends, and poker's most momentous events march in and out of fifty years of unforgettable hands. Sit side-by-side with Doyle as he replays the excitement and life-changing moments of the most thrilling and crucial hands in the history of poker: from his early games as a rounder in the rough-and-tumble "Wild West" years—where a man was more likely to get shot as he was to get a straight flush—to the nail-biting excitement of his two world championship titles. Relive million dollar hands and the high stakes tension of sidestepping police, hijackers and murderers. A thrilling collection of stories and sage poker advice. 168 pages, $14.95.

CHAMPIONSHIP NO-LIMIT & POT-LIMIT HOLD'EM *by T. J. Cloutier & Tom McEvoy.* New edition! The bible for winning pot-limit and no-limit hold'em gives you the answers to your most important questions: How do you get inside your opponents' heads and learn how to beat them at their own game? How can you tell how much to bet, raise, and reraise in no-limit hold'em? When can you bluff? How do you set up your opponents in pot-limit hold'em so that you can win a monster pot? What are the best strategies for winning no-limit and pot-limit tournaments, satellites, and supersatellites? Rock-solid and inspired advice you can bank on from two of the most recognizable figures in poker. 304 pages, $19.95.

POWERFUL WINNING POKER SIMULATIONS
A MUST FOR SERIOUS PLAYERS WITH A COMPUTER!
IBM compatible CD ROM Win 95, 98, 2000, NT, ME, XP

These incredible full color poker simulations are the best method to improve your game. Computer opponents play like real players. All games let you set the limits and rake and have fully programmable players, plus stat tracking, and Hand Analyzer for starting hands. Mike Caro, the world's foremost poker theoretician says, "Amazing... a steal for under $500... get it, it's great." Includes free phone support. "Smart Advisor" gives expert advice for every play!

NEW! Windows Versions More Features!

1. TURBO TEXAS HOLD'EM FOR WINDOWS - $59.95. Choose which players, and how many (2-10) you want to play, create loose/tight games, and control check-raising, bluffing, position, sensitivity to pot odds, and more! Also, instant replay, pop-up odds, Professional Advisor keeps track of play statistics. Free bonus: Hold'em Hand Analyzer analyzes all 169 pocket hands in detail and their win rates under any conditions you set. Caro says this "hold'em software is the most powerful ever created." Great product!

2. TURBO SEVEN-CARD STUD FOR WINDOWS - $59.95. Create any conditions of play; choose number of players (2-8), bet amounts, fixed or spread limit, bring-in method, tight/loose conditions, position, reaction to board, number of dead cards, and stack deck to create special conditions. Features instant replay. Terrific stat reporting includes analysis of starting cards, 3-D bar charts, and graphs. Play interactively and run high speed simulation to test strategies. Hand Analyzer analyzes starting hands in detail. Wow!

3. TURBO OMAHA HIGH-LOW SPLIT FOR WINDOWS - $59.95. Specify any playing conditions; betting limits, number of raises, blind structures, button position, aggressiveness/ passiveness of opponents, number of players (2-10), types of hands dealt, blinds, position, board reaction, and specify flop, turn, and river cards! Choose opponents and use provided point count or create your own. Statistical reporting, instant replay, pop-up odds high speed simulation to test strategies, amazing Hand Analyzer, and much more!

4. TURBO OMAHA HIGH FOR WINDOWS - $59.95. Same features as above, but tailored for Omaha High only. Caro says program is "an electrifying research tool...it can clearly be worth thousands of dollars to any serious player. A must for Omaha High players.

5. TURBO 7 STUD 8 OR BETTER - $59.95. Brand new with all the features you expect from the Wilson Turbo products: the latest artificial intelligence, instant advice and exact odds, play versus 2-7 opponents, enhanced data charts that can be exported or printed, the ability to fold out of turn and immediately go to the next hand, ability to peek at opponents hand, optional warning mode that warns you if a play disagrees with the advisor, and automatic mode that runs up to 50 tests unattended. Tough computer players vary their styles for a great game.

---

6. TOURNAMENT TEXAS HOLD'EM - $39.95

Set-up for tournament practice and play, this realistic simulation pits you against celebrity look-alikes. Tons of options let you control tournament size with 10 to 300 entrants, select limits, ante, rake, blind structures, freezeouts, number of rebuys and competition level of opponents. Pop-up status report shows how you're doing vs. the competition. Save tournaments in progress to play again later. Additional feature allows quick folds on finished hands.